World Affairs
and
National
Politics

World Affairs
and
National Politics

and the High Calling of God in Christ Jesus

Clyde L. Pilkington, Jr.

www.ClydePilkington.com

BIBLE STUDENT'S PRESS™
Windber, Pennsylvania

World Affairs and National Politics
and the High Calling of God in Christ Jesus
by Clyde L. Pilkington, Jr.
Copyright © 2012 by Clyde L. Pilkington, Jr.
All rights reserved.

Original Printing:
Individual articles published in the *Bible Student's Notebook,* ©1998-2012

Second Printing:
First book edition, 1996, under the title: *Human Government: Where Do We Fit In?*

Third Printing:
Second book edition, 2012

Executive Editor: André Sneidar
Associate Editors: Richard Lemons; Nadine Sneidar
Layout and Design: Great Adventure in Faith

Cover design by Clyde L. Pilkington, III

ISBN-10:   1-934251-91-7
ISBN-13:   978-1-934251-91-1

Published by

Bible Student's Press™
An imprint of *Pilkington & Sons*
P.O. Box 265
Windber, PA 15963

For other titles by the author, visit
www.ClydePilkington.com

For information on *Bible Student's Press*™ releases, visit
www.BibleStudentsPress.com

For information on other Bible study resources, visit
www.StudyShelf.com

Printed in the United States of America.

DEDICATED TO ...

The members of Christ's Body who, over the past two millennia, have, in spite of tremendous opposition and trial, faithfully carried out their ambassadorship outside of nationalism.

CONTENTS

Acknowledgements

Honor all men (I Peter 2:17).

Anyone who really knows me, knows that I have always been a gleaner by nature. Over the years I have collected many resources for this important project.

I would love to *honor* the many authors who have helped me in my own personal journey. I do this by including excerpts that have spoken to me on some level regarding this subject. Since each of us have a different background and are on a unique journey designed by Father, you may not enjoy some of the segments as much as others; but I do trust that, overall, you will find their inclusion a help, as they have been to me.

I have made an honest effort to share my sources correctly, but since this work has spanned over two decades, I would like to apologize sincerely beforehand for any oversight in properly acknowledging any resource. I will provide appropriate corrections in future editions if and as I am made aware of any inadvertent lack of recognition.

Although a handful of quotations are from beloved and trusted sources, more often than not I do not always particularly endorse the authors or books from which the quotations are taken. Sometimes, when I am reading, it is simply amazing to me how a certain author can admit in print to some grand truth that their writings otherwise generally deny. For the authors of these quotes, the truth that is conveyed by them may seem oddly "out of place"; but in some ways, the more unlikely the source, the more amazingly it seems to me to testify of the truth, and how God can get it said even through them – after all, even Paul went so far as to quote a pagan poet on Mars' Hill.

Many of the quotations are edited and abridged for brevity, as well as grammatical and scriptural clarity.

Preface

Let every man abide in the same calling wherein he was called (I Corinthians 7:20).

All have a calling of sorts, some of which are very specific, some more general.

Israel and the Body of Christ have distinct callings: one is earthly, the other is heavenly. Even within Israel and the Body of Christ's callings, there were and are individually specific callings. Paul, for example, was not only a member of the Body of Christ, but he was also called to be its Apostle. Others were teachers, encouragers, hospitable hosts, financial contributors, etc. – all called to fellowship with Paul, assisting him in his work.

Adversaries have a divine calling as well: Pharaoh (Roman 9:17), Cyrus (Isaiah 45:1), Judas (John 13:27)[1] and, of course, *the* great Adversary Satan – all are Father's instruments.

From the Divine viewpoint (the absolute), even the seemingly "un-called" have been "called" to their place and task in life – some as active pawns of *the* Adversary, most just the backdrop for the stage of good *and* evil. *All* play their precise and vital role at the direction of the Sovereign Placer and Subjector.[2] All is *of* God. All is *from* Him, all is *through* Him, all is circulating back *to* Him, that He may be *"All in all."* If we really believe this it will change our worldview. Early in my Christian life I was a political activist, serving

---

1. See the author's work, *Judas: God's Overlooked Servant.*
2. The basic Hebrew word used for God is *"El."* The word means "Placer," "Subjector."

as a political party youth chairman, coordinating party functions and even working the polls for numerous local, state and national elections.

A little over twenty years ago I began to see my role *very* differently in relationship to the power-play scheme perpetuated by the influence of the religious-political world system. The course of this world is currently designed by God to demonstrate mankind's folly apart from Him. He has therefore subjected it under the dominion of the *"god of this world"* (II Corinthians 4:4), Satan giving governmental power (relatively) to *"whomever he will"* (Luke 4:5-6).

As believers we are not of *this* world – we are strangers and foreigners here. Our citizenship is in heaven (Philippians 3:20); our King is the Lord Jesus Christ (I Timothy 1:17; 6:15); and we are His ambassadors in a foreign land (II Corinthians 5:20). Ours is *"the high calling of God in Christ Jesus"* (Philippians 3:14).

Writing to Understand

My motivation in writing was not so much to be understood as it was to understand.

Henry Hudson
Magna Carta of the Kingdom

Introduction

The Most High rules in the kingdom of men, and gives it to whomever He will (Daniel 4:17, 25).

This book is an important one for me, and has been over fifteen-years in the making.

In 1996 I published a preliminary work entitled, *Human Government: Where Do We Fit In?* For the past three U.S. Presidential election years, I had desired to publish an enlargement of it. Father, of course, knowing better than I, had other plans. Although the main thrust of this new book is the same, the ensuing years have added great fullness and dimension to it.

Presidential elections, as with *all* other aspects of nationalism, are Father's demonstration – pressing on our hearts – of the folly of mankind outside of Him. So many are franticly, passionately, and yet vainly involved in their search for a national savior. I should know – I used to play my own active role in the process.

To me, Father's humor appears to come shining through more than ever this year. As I write these words there are three leading candidates contending for President Obama's seat. "Politics makes strange bedfellows," certainly applies in this situation. It is so amusing to watch "Evangelical Christians" busy courting two Roman Catholics and a Mormon to save them from a President with a "Muslim" past. I can't help but chuckle every time I think of it.

It is my prayer to Father that the reader of these pages will find some direction and comfort in the words that follow. These truths contained in this book certainly have done so for me.

As A.E. Knoch (1874-1965) wrote regarding his own series on God and the Nations,

> We hope that everyone who reads these lines will experience the immense relief which comes only with a realization that the world at the present time, with all its frightfullness and frustration, is just as God intended it to be. He foretold its failure and is using it to humble His creatures and prepare them for their destiny.

Unsearchable Riches
Volume 36, 1945

Indeed, Father is preparing us for our destiny, and for us, it is time to embrace that destiny – our celestial calling.

My books never seem to be "finished." Every time that I re-read my own writings I inevitably see something that I would add or change. Lord willing, there will be future editions of this book, and as one author has well stated,

I don't know if every writer on the things of the Spirit

has the same problem – no sooner have I completed one manuscript than I see this and this and this which could be put much more clearly, or whole areas of insights which should be added. I feel like the automobile dealers who *must* produce a new model each year![1]

Clyde

Clyde L. Pilkington, Jr.
Windber, PA
April 2012

---

1. Norman Grubb (1895-1993), *God Unlimited.*

God tested mankind for much more than a millennium up to the deluge, before they formed nations and were organized into political units.

A.E. Knoch (1874-1965)
Unsearchable Riches
Volume 36, 1945

Chapter 1

Dominion

*I*n Genesis chapter one God gave dominion to Adam and Eve.

*God said, "Let us make man in our image, after our likeness: and **let them have dominion** over the fish of the sea, and over the fowl of the air, and over the cattle, and over all the earth, and over every creeping thing that creeps upon the earth"* (Genesis 1:27).

DOMINION OF FAMILY

The dominion of the earth was vested in the family. The authorities were a husband and his wife. The perpetuation and increase in their domain *were* to be *through* their children.

*God blessed them, and God said to them, "Be fruitful, and multiply, and replenish the earth, and subdue it: and have **dominion** over the fish of the sea, and over the fowl of the air, and over every living thing that moves on the earth"* (Genesis 1:28).

God gave dominion to Adam and Eve (:26); but note (:28) that the subduing of, and continued dominion over the earth, followed *"be fruitful, and multiply, and replenish the earth."* As Adam and Eve had children, their dominion increased and the authority naturally passed to them.

Thus the dominion of the earth was vested in the *family*. This is not in the nuclear family[1] of contemporary Western culture, but in the family by the patriarchal system.[2] This form of dominion was, by natural and general rule, passed to and through the eldest son, the first born.[3]

---

1. "The Old Testament family is a wider circle than the typical two-generation nuclear family of parents and children characteristic of contemporary Western society." Sinclair Ferguson, ed., *New Dictionary of Theology* (Downers Grove, IL, InterVarsity Press, 1988), page 251.

    "Another term for family, *'bayith'*, included *all* living within the confines and jurisdiction of the dwelling." Merrel Tenney, ed., *New International Dictionary of the Bible* (Grand Rapids, MI, Zondervan, 1987), page 343.

    "In both Testaments the family is much broader, and much more important, than we normally see it being in our day. With regard to the family, one thing is absolutely clear in the Bible. Nowhere in Scripture is there found the idea that each 'family' consists of two parents and 2.3 children living in a house on a lot 100 by 60 feet and as an isolated unit, with 'King and Queen' and a three-bedroom home as their little 'castle.' In the Bible, the family was *too broad* and *too important* for such isolation ...

    "Actually, the concept of the 'nuclear' family of today – the typical two generation nuclear family of parents and children characteristic of contemporary Western society – is not only foreign to the Bible; it is relatively new in the history of America as well ..." Terry & Beverly Miethe, *Serving Christ: A Family Affair* (Joplin, MO, College Press, 1995) pages 178-179.

2. Patriarchal – "Belonging to patriarchs," Patriarch – "The father and ruler of a family; one who governs by paternal right." Noah Webster, *American Dictionary of the English Language*, 1828.

    "Under the patriarchal administration, the father is supreme in command. The authority which the father has extends to his wife, to his children, his children's children, his servants, and to all his household, and if he is the sheik, to all the tribe ... When Abraham, Isaac and Jacob lived in tents in the Land of Promise, they were ruled by this same system ... In many ways the father was the supreme court of appeal in domestic matters." Fred H. Wight, *Manners and Customs of Bible Lands* (Chicago, IL, Moody Press), page 103.

3. "In a majority of cases, the great authority which the father had was handed down to his eldest son, who took over the position of leadership upon the death of his father. Hence Isaac became the new 'sheik' over his father's household upon the death of Abraham ... In some cases, the father bestowed the succession of authority on other than the eldest son,

Family dominion continued all the way through to Noah and his sons, as the original command to Adam and Eve was *repeated* to them:

God blessed Noah and his sons, and said to them, "Be fruitful, and multiply, and replenish the earth" (Genesis 9:1).

> The history of nations is a history of failure,
>
> — A.E. Knoch

To assist Noah and his sons in curtailing the widespread corruption on the earth, God gave this patriarchal dominion the authority to execute the ultimate penalty that could be inflicted: death.

Surely your blood of your lives will I require; at the hand of every beast will I require it, and at the hand of man; at the hand of every man's brother will I require the life of man. Whoever sheds man's blood, by man shall his blood be shed: for in the image of God He made man. And you, be you fruitful, and multiply; bring forth abundantly in the earth, and multiply therein (Genesis 9:5-7).

Thus family dominion continued for nearly two thousand years before the introduction of nationalism.[4]

---

as when Isaac bestowed it upon Jacob instead of Esau (Genesis 27)" Wight, page 104.

4. We can roughly determine the time between Adam and the Babel from a set of genealogies found in Scripture, that ends with a man named Peleg. We take the years between a father and the birth of his son, as recorded in Scripture, then adding these numbers together, we can acquire the approximate date.

In Genesis 5:1 we learn that Adam was 130 years old when his son Seth was born. In :6 we find out that Seth was 105 when his son Enosh was born. We continue this process through the genealogies until we arrive at Noah (:1-32):

THE REBELLIOUS FEDERATION OF DOMINION

God had given clear instruction to *"replenish the earth ... and bring forth abundantly in the earth."* Yet, instead of spreading out in the earth to *"replenish ... abundantly in the earth,"* man did the very opposite.

> *The whole earth ... said, "Go to, let us build us a city and a tower, whose top may reach into heaven; and let us make us a name, lest we be scattered abroad on the face of the whole earth." And the LORD came down to see the city and the tower which the children of men built. And the LORD said, "Behold, the people is one, and they have*

Adam to Seth - 130 years
Seth to Enosh - 105 years
Enosh to Kenan - 90 yeas
Kenan to Mahalalel - 70 years
Mahalalel to Jared - 65 years
Jared to Enoch - 162 years
Enoch to Methuselah - 65 years
Methuselah to Lamech - 187 years
Lamech to Noah - 182 years
From Adam to Noah we have a calculation of 1056 years.

Then in Genesis 7:6 we learn that Noah was 600 at the time of the flood. So adding 600 to 1056, we come up the date 1656 years between creation and the flood. Continuing with the genealogies found in Genesis 5:32, we see that Noah had three sons: Shem, Ham and Japheth. From here we move forward to Genesis 11:10-16 and continue with the genealogy of Shem.

Adam to the Flood - 1656 years
Flood to Arphaxad - 2 years
Arphaxad to Shelah - 35 years
Shelah to Eber - 30 years
Eber to Peleg - 34 years

This brings us to 1757 years after creation. The Scriptures tell us that in the days of Peleg the earth was divided (Genesis 10:25; *cf.* I Chronicles 1:19). In fact, the name "Peleg" means "division." It was during Peleg's lifetime that the people of the earth were divided into different language groups and dispersed. Going to Genesis 11:18-19 we can find out how long he lived.

Peleg to Reu - 30 years
Reu to Peleg's death - 209

Peleg born approximately 1757 years after Adam was created, and lived for 239 years. This places his death 1996 years after Adam was created, making the Tower of Babel, according to the scriptural account, somewhere between 1757 and 1996 years after Adam was created.

all one language; and this they begin to do: and now nothing will be restrained from them, which they have imagined to do. Go to, let us go down, and there confound their language, that they may not understand one another's speech." So the LORD *scattered them abroad from there on the face of all the earth: and they left off to build* [quit, or stopped building] *the city. Therefore is the name of it called Babel; because the* LORD *did there confound the language of all the earth: and from there did the* LORD *scatter them abroad on the face of all the earth* (Genesis 11:1, 4-9).

FEDERALISM PRODUCED THE FIRST CITY AND FIRST WAR

In the rebellious attempt to federate their God-given patriarchal dominion we find the first city established – *"let us build us a city."* Of course, once true patriarchy is abandoned for a coalition, it would not take long for such a federation to institute war, since it is easier to send other men's sons to battle than your own.

> Even when withstanding God's will we are fulfilling His intention,
>
> — A.E. Knoch

*It came to pass in the days of Amraphel king of Shinar, Arioch king of Ellasar, Chedorlaomer king of Elam, and Tidal king of nations; that **these made war** with Bera king of Sodom, and with Birsha king of Gomorrah, Shinab king of Admah, and Shemeber king of Zeboiim, and the king of Bela, which is Zoar. All these were joined together in the vale of Siddim, which is the Salt Sea* (Genesis 14:1-3).

John Phillips writes,

> The story of Babel shows how man used his new-found
> authority to plan organized rebellion against the very
> throne of God itself. Up until this time rebellion had been
> on an *individual* basis, now it had become *federated*. The
> world's first "united nations," with headquarters at Baby-
> lon, symbolized the last one. Genesis 11 and 12 foreshad-
> ow Revelation 13, 17-18.[5]

---

5. John Phillips, *Exploring Romans* (Neptune, NJ, Loizeaux Brothers, 1969), p.
   213.

It is not God's object to fill the world with peace at the present time. It will help us in the terrible time we are going through to realize this. God wants to teach man that **he cannot rule apart from Him.** Man is made to rule and he is going to rule, but he is not able apart from the Deity.

A.E. Knoch (1874-1965)
Unsearchable Riches
Volume 36, 1945

Chapter 2

Nationalism

Why do the nations rage? (Psalm 2:1; Acts 4:25).

The English word "nation" is a translation of various Hebrew and Greek words (such as *gowy* in Psalm 2:1, and *ethnos* in Acts 4:25) which are also used to translate such words as *"Gentiles"* and *"heathen"* in many English Bibles.[1] The key to nationalism has to do with understanding its place in God's plan. When one understands God's purposes they are better able to know how to relate to them. Nationalism is a divine judgment on mankind introduced at Babel[2] (Genesis 10, 11), and is His instrument of vanity; for, truly, *"the nations rage, and the people imagine a **vain** thing"* (Psalm 2:1; Acts 4:25).

Twice, very specifically, we are told in Scripture that it was during the life of Peleg that *the earth was divided* (Genesis 10:25; *cf.* I Chronicles 1:19). In fact, the name Peleg means "division." It was during his lifetime, at Babel, that the people of the earth were divided into different language groups and dispersed.

---

1. "But in the Scriptures I think the meaning is very clear ... You will notice that I always translate *'nation'* or *'nations,'* when I know very well I could make more ear-tickling, flowing English by saying *'gentiles'* or *'heathen.'"* – A.E. Knoch, What is a Nation? *Unsearchable Riches*, Volume 36, 1946
2. "When did nations commence? At Babel." – A.E. Knoch, What is a Nation?, *Unsearchable Riches*, Volume 36, 1946

God's judgment on the rebellion of mankind's federation of their family dominion was the introduction of nationalism. Up until this point all mankind was of one language. At Babel God multiplies their languages, forcing them to scatter in division. These divisions governed as regional political alliances (*i.e.*, nations). A.E. Knoch defines a nation as "an *organic political unity.*"[3]

> The history of the world is but the breaking of governments, systems, ideals and programs.
> — M.R. DeHann

Nationalism is but a further tool in God's hand to subject mankind to vanity (Romans 8:20).[4] Men look to their governments for the answer to their problems, and even Christians try in *vain* to influence the predestined course of the nations. The history of nationalism is one of successive failure. Hopes are raised for a "good" government, only to find that "evil" prevails once again: one nation after another, one kingdom overthrowing another, one party defeating another, one cause overpowering another, all in vain cycles. God is at the center of it all, *"for there is no power but of God: the powers that be are ordained of God"* (Romans 13:1). Pharaoh

---

3. A.E. Knoch, "What is a Nation?," *Unsearchable Riches*, Volume 36, 1946
4. The Greek word translated *"vanity"* here is *mataiotēs*, and is defined by Joseph Thayer (*Thayer's Greek-English Lexicon of the New Testament*) as: "What is devoid of truth and appropriateness; perverseness, depravity, frailty, want [*i.e.*, lack] of vigor." B.W. Johnson (*People's New Testament*) defines it as "seeking without finding."

It is translated in the follow ways by various versions:

"*aimless frustration*" (*An Understandable Version*)
"*spoiled*" (*Bible in Worldwide English*)
"*frustrated*" (*Goodspeed New Testament*)
"*imperfection*" (*Montgomery New Testament*)
"*folly*" (*The Riverside New Testament*)
"*failure and unreality*"(*Weymouth New Testament*)
"*futile*"(*Moffat New Testament*)
"*weak*" (*New Life Study Testament*)
"*imperfection*" (*Centenary Translation*)
"*dissolution*" (*Original New Testament*)

was God's servant (Romans 9:17), as well as was Cyrus (Isaiah 45:1).

This of course means that we must never forget that *"the most High rules in the kingdom of men, and gives it to whomever He will"* (Daniel 4:17, 25), and that *"He does according to His will ... among the inhabitants of the earth: and none can restrain His hand"* (Daniel 4:35). It is God Who rules *"over all the kingdoms of the nations"* (II Chronicles 20:6).

We know that *"the king's heart is in the hand of the Lord, as the rivers of water: He turns it wherever He will"* (Proverbs 21:1), and in fact, *"... HE is a great King over all the earth"* (Psalm 47:2).

God rules over *all* nations, establishing their times and boundaries. The who, how, when and where are *all* determined by Him for His Own purposes.

> [God] *has made of one blood all nations of men for to dwell on all the face of the earth, and has determined the times before appointed, and the bounds of their habitation* (Act 17:26).

Satan currently has been appointed the *"god of this age"* (II Corinthians 4:4). God uses him as an instrument to set up and remove the kingdoms and the rulers of the world to fulfill His divine purpose of the ages.

> Evil must needs be, and God controls it so as to accomplish His beneficent purpose.
>
> — A.E. Knoch

> [God] *changes the times and the seasons: He removes kings, and sets up kings* (Daniel 2:21).

The most High rules in the kingdom of men, and gives it to whomever He will (Daniel 4:17, 25, 32; 5:21).

God controls the wheels of government and the counsels of kings to bring about His own great designs.
— C.H. Mackintosh

It is God Who directs the affairs of this earth, including the political realm, and He uses the instrumentality of the Adversary to accomplish His purpose among the nations, bringing them all to vanity.

Let them be confounded and troubled for the future; yes, let them be put to shame, and perish: that men may know that You, Whose name alone is Jehovah, are the most high over all the earth (Psalm 83:17-18).

All the inhabitants of the earth are reputed as nothing: and [God] *does according to His will in the army of heaven, and among the inhabitants of the earth: and none can stay His hand, or say to Him, "What have You done?"* (Daniel 4:35).

Thus the Lord Jesus Christ said to Pilate,

You could have no power at all against Me, except it were given you from above (John 19:11).

THE KINGDOMS OF THE WORLD

The Adversary, taking Him up into a high mountain, showed to Him all the kingdoms of the world in a moment of time. The Adversary said to Him, "All this power will I give You, and the glory of them: for that is delivered to me; and to whomever I will I give it. If You therefore will worship me, all will be Yours (Luke 4:5-7).

Gregory A. Boyd writes concerning this passage.

In Luke 4 the Adversary tempted Jesus by showing Him *"all the kingdoms of the world"* while saying, *"All this power will I give You, and the glory of them: for that is delivered to me; and to whomsoever I will I give it.* Jesus, of course, would not worship the Adversary to acquire these kingdoms; but note: He doesn't dispute the Adversary's claim to own them.

Apparently, the authority of all of the kingdoms of the world has been given to Satan. It's not clear from this text whether we humans gave the Adversary this authority when we surrendered to him in the Garden (Genesis 3) or whether God originally entrusted him with this authority. What is clear is that, however it came about, God's cosmic archenemy now owns the authority of all versions of the kingdoms of the world and gives this authority to whomever he pleases.

This teaching is found in various forms throughout the New Testament. This kingdom is symbolized as *"Babylon."* Certainly, some governments are better than others; but no earthly kingdom, however good, is exempt from the scriptural teaching that it is a part of *"Babylon,"* a worldwide kingdom ruled by Satan.

> All knowledge is relative: it is based on contrast.
> — A.E. Knoch

Along these lines, Jesus three times refers to Satan as the *"prince* [ruler] *of this world"* (John 12:31; 14:30; 16:11). The term *"prince* [ruler]*"* was a political one used to denote the highest ruling authority in a given region – and Jesus applied it to Satan over the whole world! Functionally, Satan is the acting CEO of all earthly governments. Paul agrees, for he refers to Satan as *"the god* [magistrate] *of this world"* (II Corinthians 4:4) and as *"the prince* [ruler] *of the power of the air"* (Ephesians 2:2).

Gregory A. Boyd
The Myth of a Christian Nation (2005)
Pages 21-22

A.E. Knoch writes,

God is "trying" a great number – I should not say of *experiments* – but a vast variety of *demonstrations* to shut man's mouth;[5] so that he cannot say that he has not had a fair opportunity to prove that he can govern apart from God. ... Apart from all being subject to God there cannot be and *should not* be a perfect government.

A.E. Knoch (1874-1965)
Unsearchable Riches
Volume 38, 1947

GOD'S PURPOSE IN HUMAN GOVERNMENT

> Patriotism is just a national religion, no different from other religious systems.
> — André Sneidar

God, in His wise and loving sovereignty, is teaching us that mankind does not have the ability to govern itself apart from Him. He *did* create man to rule, and he surely will one day, but he will never be able to do it successfully apart from Him. This is the divine lesson of hu-

---

5. *"... that every mouth may be shut and all the world made answerable to God"* (Romans 3:19, *James Moffatt*).

man government, and He leaves no stone unturned in teaching us this lesson. There will be no excuse[6] that man did not have a fair try. In the end, God will have amply demonstrated that under *any and all* circumstances, no matter how favorable, mankind was not able to manage his own affairs successfully without God.

Man has failed at family and national rule. He has failed at religious and secular rule. No matter what economic form: capitalism, socialism, or

> The event of things, predicted many ages before ... is a convincing argument that the world is governed by providence.
> — Sir Isaac Newton

communism; no matter what administrative form: dictatorship, totalitarian, theocracy, monarchy, parliamentary, republic, or anarchy; no matter what authoritative form: revolutionary, aristocracy, or democracy – they all have the same end: *utter failure without Him.*

It is interesting how God has taken mankind through various cycles of government throughout different periods of human history, and that the last-ditch effort by humanity has been "a government of the people, by the people, and for the people,"[7] which also is destined to absolute disaster. Mankind may have balked at all former attempts to have *others rule over them,* but in the end they will not even be able to govern themselves. Yes, even the "Great American Experiment" will end in complete ruin.

THE FUTILITY OF HUMAN GOVERNMENT

In every detail of the long and sordid history of nationalism, God is building a grand contrast to His glorious Kingdom of

---

6. *"... so that they are without excuse"* (Romans 1:20).
7. Abraham Lincoln, *The Gettysburg Address.*

righteousness – one that will encompass all of His creation, in the heavens and on the earth. What a transcendent contrast that will be!

This will be accomplished by the only appointed King of kings, Lord of lords, and Prince of peace: Jesus Christ.[8]

As believers, God's first-fruit, we have the wonderful privilege of seeing this contrast early. Paul tells us that God has already

> *Delivered us from the dominion of darkness, and has transferred us into the Kingdom of His dear Son* (Colossians 1:13).

Nationalism is but the "*jurisdiction of darkness*,"[9] but we are thankful that we have been "*transported*"[10] out of it, and into His Kingdom. We now have "*our citizenship ... in heaven; from where also we look for the Savior, the Lord Jesus Christ*" (Philippians 3:20).

---

8. See Appendix 6: *The True Basis of World Peace*
9. *Concordant Literal New Testament.*
10. *Concordant Literal New Testament.*

A man has a desert ranch of large extent. He is told it is worthless as pasturage or farming land. He fences off twelve acres; breaks it, harrows it, fertilizes it, cultivates it, and reaps only sagebrush and cactus!

Israel was God's twelve acres. He gave them His law, instructed them, disciplined them, warned them, restrained them, protected them, and sent His Son to them; and Him they rejected and crucified. In this act the Gentiles [i.e., Nations] joined.

All are under the judgment of God. There is no use of a further test. There is nothing in the flesh for God. Man is utterly unable to retrieve his condition.

H.A. Ironside (1878-1951)
Lectures on the Epistle to the Romans

Chapter 3

God's Nation

Its Establishment and Fall

I will make of you a great nation (Genesis 12:2).

t Babel God gave up mankind to the vanity of nationalism, setting them aside as His *primary* instruments, and turned to the establishment of a single new nation that would (eventually) be His contrast to all other nations.

Human government, as all other endeavors *"under the sun"* (by those who still find their identity in Adam), is *"full of evil"* (Ecclesiastes 9:3). In other words, the nations of the world are now under Satanic assignment.

A NEW DIVINELY ESTABLISHED NATION

What follows the account of the rebellion of federation at Babel is the selection of another man, and another new dominion. The man is Abram, later called Abraham. God chose him to establish a new nation, a new nationality of people:

Now the LORD had said to Abram, "Get out of your country, and from your kindred, and from your father's *house, to a land that I will show you: and I will make of you a great **nation** ..."* (Genesis 12:1-2).

God's ultimate plan is to bless all other nations through the instrumentality of Abraham's nation.[1] Note very carefully how the rest of the text is phrased:

*I will bless you, and make your name great and you will be a blessing: and I will bless them who bless you, and curse him who curses you: and in you shall **all families of the earth** be blessed* (:2-3).

Notice that this phrase *"all families of the earth"* is repeated in Genesis 28:14.

*Thy seed shall be as the dust of the earth, and you will spread abroad to the west, to the east, to the north, to the south: and in you and in your seed shall **all families of the earth** be blessed.*

Yet notice in other passages this promise is phrased differently:

*In your seed will all the **nations of the earth be blessed;** because you have obeyed My voice* (Genesis 22:18).

I will make your seed to multiply as the stars of heaven, and will give to your seed all these countries; and

---

1. "God prepared for a new nation through the seed of Abraham. He had a threefold purpose with this nation: (1) to be the *channel* for the incoming *seed of the woman* who would restore to man the dominion of the earth, under the headship of God. (2) As a *repository* for His truth in the earth, as we read in Romans 3:1-2, and then, (3) as a *national witness* to Himself before the nations of the earth, that had turned from Him. The nation Israel always being a promise of better things to come on this earth, even as all the prophets witness." Eugene F. Rueweler. *A Dispensational & Prophetic Bible Study That Answers the Question WHY WAR?* (St. Louis Daily Radio Bible Class, n.d.) p. 10.

*in your seed will **all the nations of the earth** be blessed* (Genesis 26:4).

Did you notice the difference? The word *"families"* was replaced by the word *"nations."* This is not just an English change: the same is true of the Hebrew. God considers the words *"nations"* and *"families"* to be interchangeable on this point.

Therefore, notice *"the **nation** of Israel"* is called also *"the **children** of Israel,"* and *"the **house** of Israel."*

Israel was also further broken down by families: *"the **twelve tribes** of Israel."*

Of course, *"Israel"* was the changed name of *"Jacob"*:

> *He said, "Your name will not be called Jacob any more, but Israel: for as a prince have you power with God and with men, and have prevailed"* (Genesis 32:28).

So, when we speak of the nation of Israel, we speak of Jacob's nation, the children of Jacob, the household of Jacob (*i.e.,* his descendants). Jacob was the patriarch of Israel. The nation was divided into smaller family clans or tribes, named after their chief patriarchs[2] (*e.g.* tribe of Judah). In Scripture even *the nation of Egypt* is called *"the family of Egypt"* (Zechariah 14:18).

The subdivision of the government of Israel's descendants did not stop there. The tribes were divided additionally into smaller branches of governmental authority by family, for example:

> *"The family of the Amramites"* (Numbers 3:27)
> are *"the Amramites"* (I Chronicles 26:23) and,

---

2. *"Jacob begot the twelve patriarchs"* (Acts 7:8).

"The family of the Izeharites" (Numbers 3:27)
    are *"the Izeharites"* (I Chronicles 26:23) and,

"The family of the Hebronites" (Numbers 3:27: 26:58)
    are *"the Hebronites"* (I Chronicles 26:23) and,

"The family of the Uzzielites" (Numbers 3:27)
    are *"the Uzzielites"* (I Chronicles 26:23) and,

"The family of the Gileadites" (Numbers 26:29)
    are *"the Gileadites"* (Judges 12:5) and,

"The family of the Gershonites" (Numbers 26:57)
    are *"the Gershonites"* (I Chronicles 23:7) and,

"The family of the Kohathites" (Numbers 26:57)
    are *"the Kohathites"* (Numbers 10:21) and,

"The family of Judah" (Joshua 7:17)
    are *"Judah"* (Joshua 18:5) and,

"The family of the Zarhites" (Joshua 7:17)
    are *"the Zarhites"* (I Chronicles 27:11) and,

"The family of the Danites" (Judges 13:2)
    are *"the Danites"* (I Chronicles 12:35), etc.

These smaller governmental family groups were led by the family elders. Our English word "elder" comes from the German *eltern* which means "parents."[3] In fact, Coverdale translated Romans 1:30, *"Disobedient to their elders."* The elders were the older, senior, mature men of the families (*i.e.*, grandfathers).[4] What we are talking about is the natural and

---

3. Richard Chenevix Trench. *Dictionary of Obsolete English* (New York: Philosophical Library, 1958), p. 83.
4. The Hebrew word translated *"elders"* is defined by Strong (#2205) as *"old."* The KJV translators also rendered the word as *"ancient men"* (Ezra

national ministry of grandfathers.[5]

3:12), *"aged"* (Job 12:20), *"eldest"* (Genesis 24:2), *"old"* (Genesis 18:12), *"senators"* (Psalm 105:22, from which we get our word "senior") and *"utterly old"* (Ezekiel 9:6).

"The term *'elders'* was no doubt originally applied to the heads of families, to the oldest persons in tribes." James M. Freeman, *Manners & Customs of the Bible* (Springdale, PA: Whitaker, 1996), p. 387.

"Elder, literally, an older man." William C. Martin, editor. *The Layman's Bible Encyclopedia* (Nashville, TN: Southwestern, 1964), P. 214.

"The basic meaning of the Hebrew and Greek words for elder is *'old age.'* Herbert Lockyer, editor, *Nelson's Illustrated Bible Dictionary* (Nashville TN: Thomas Nelson, 1986), p. 330.

An elder is one who "had by virtue of his right as firstborn succeeded to the headship of a father's house, of a tribal family, or of the tribe itself (I Kings 8:1-3; Judges 8:14, 16). In the ordinary course of nature only men of mature age came into these positions, hence the designation elder." J.D. Davis, *Illustrated Davis Dictionary of the Bible* (Nashville, TN: Royal Publishers, 1898-1973), p. 211.

5. Parents are parents for life, and the covering they provide for their offspring grows ever larger. The honor due them by their children is one which includes their legacy. As men grow older, they become exalted fathers, the fathers of fathers. In ancient Israel, each allotment of land had a village – a cluster of houses where there lived an extended family group (3-5 generations), with their servants, hired hands, and their families. Each man was the head of his respective household, but the over-all magistrate for that estate and of all who lived upon it was the leading male member. Generally, that male was the oldest father who was the heir to the land. His word was final. It was he who went to the city gates to convene with the other elders as the family spokesman.

Of course, the Grandpa was not to be a tyrant or a despot. If he was, biblical laws had ways of dealing with his sins. He did not meddle in the affairs of his grown children or of residents, as a rule. He supervised the affairs of the estate. He had eminent dominion. Primarily, though, he was there for consultation and to sit as a judge in family disputes. The goal of Hebrew education was to train children for dominion over their own estates. The training did not end at age 18. It was a gradual process of transference of power.

Grandpa had appellate jurisdiction within the family structure, and he was the spokesman and elector for the family at the city gate. The village eldership was not subservient to the city eldership. Much like the equal suffrage of the several States in the Unites States Senate, they each stood on equal footing, irrespective of the populations of their constituent bodies.

The link between the private government of the family in the home and on the family estate with the outside world is the eldership of the grandfather. — James Wesley Stivers, *Restoring the Foundations: Essays in Relational Theology,* Patriarch Publishing House (2007), pp. 59-60

WHY ISRAEL?

God's plan with Israel is to make them a blessing to the nations. They were to be, and one day *will* be, His channel of relationship with the earth.

> *The nations will come to your light, and kings to the brightness of your rising* (Isaiah 60:3).

This ultimately will be fulfilled through their promised Messiah:

> *Unto us a Child is born, unto us a Son is given: and the **government** will be on His shoulder ... Of the increase of His government and peace there will be no end, on the throne of David, and on his kingdom, to order it, and to establish it with judgment and with justice lasting for the age. The zeal of the Lord of hosts will perform this* (Isaiah 9:6-7).

When the Lord Jesus Christ came, He was Israel's *national* hope:

> *The angel said to her, "Fear not, Mary, for you have found favor with God. Behold, you will conceive in your womb, and bring forth a son, and will call His name Jesus. He will be great, and will be called the Son of the Highest: and the Lord God will give to Him the throne of His Father David: And He will reign over the house of Jacob* (Luke 1:30-33).

This passage is significant. Israel, at the time of the birth of Christ, although in their own land, had lost their governmental control to another nation. They were occupied by a foreign army. Yet, instead of rejoicing over their long awaited Messiah, they rejected Him, choosing instead the rule of Rome over them:

We will not have this Man to reign over us (Luke 19:14).

Away with Him, away with Him, crucify Him ... We have no king but Caesar (John 19:15).

THE BABEL-PENTECOST CONNECTION

The events of Pentecost were a sign to Israel of their unbelief and impending fall. A thoughtful look will reveal the correlation between *the nations* at Babel, and *the nation of Israel* at Pentecost.

The nations eventually were set aside following the *confusion* **OF** *the languages* at Babel.

Go to, let us go down, and there confound their language, that they may not understand one another's speech (Genesis 11:7).

Israel eventually was set aside following the *confusion* **BY** *the languages* at Pentecost.

Now when this was noised abroad, the multitude came together, and were confounded, because that every man heard them speak in his own language (Acts 2:6).

Associated with the miracle of tongues at Babel was the scattering of the nations *"abroad from thence on the face of all the earth"* (Genesis 11:8).

Associated with the miracle of tongues at Pentecost were the Twelve Tribes that were *"scattered abroad."* Both events were a sign of the national judgment of God.

Both were followed by the selection of a new leader.

Babel in Genesis 11 is followed by the *separation* of Abram (whose name was later changed to Abraham) in Genesis 12.

Pentecost in Acts 2 is followed by the *separation* of Saul (whose name was later changed to Paul) in Acts 9.

The nations were alienated from God, set aside by the formation of the *one new nation.*

Now Israel was alienated from God, set aside by the formation of the *one new man.*

Israel had joined the rebellion of the nations, Stephen giving the judicial indictment of God; they were

> *Stiff-necked and uncircumcised in heart and ears* (Acts 7:51).

Israel had rejected the ministry and efforts of God (*cf.* Isaiah 6:9-10), His Son (Matthew 13:14-15), and then by His Spirit (Matthew 12:31-32). With final rejection of God's Spirit, their generation had *nationally* committed the unpardonable sin. The nation had been *"enlightened"* and had *"tasted of the heavenly gift, and were made partakers of holy Spirit."* They had *"tasted the good Word of God, and the powers of the world to come."* Yet, with all of this, they still rejected the only source of their national hope *"and put Him to an open shame."* It was now impossible for this generation to *"renew them again to repentance"* (Hebrews 6:4-6; *cf.* Acts 28:26-27).

They had rejected (1) God, (2) God's Son, (3) God's Spirit.

Three strikes and they're out! After Israel's long history with God, they had joined the nations in unbelief and rebellion.

Today, God has *no* favored nation; *all* nations of the earth are now heathen nations!

> *There is no difference: For all have sinned, and come short of the glory of God* (Romans 3:22-23).

(For a more in-depth look at Israel read the author's book *God's Holy Nation – Israel and Her Earthly Purpose.*)

The Jews want to be a nation at a time when God does not want them to be one. ... A great deal of the trouble of today is due to the fact that this nation which God does not want to have power, is trying to get it. ... It is not in accordance with the mind of God. God's time is future, but they have underground methods. I do not blame them in a way. If we had the background that they have, of being the nation that God has chosen, we would probably do likewise. ... When any body of people tries to do something contrary to God's plans, instead of being a blessing they will be a curse.

A.E. Knoch (1874-1965)
Unsearchable Riches
Volume 36, 1945

Chapter 4

Zionism

You are not My people, and I will not be your God (Hosea 1:9).

The modern-day movement of *Zionism*, and the *Israeli* nation, must *not* be confused with *scriptural Israel*.

Israel was once God's *"head"* among the nations (Deuteronomy 28:13); but as she was warned, she is *now* the *"tail"* (28:44). Instead of imparting spiritual light to the nations, Israel is now blinded (Romans 11:25). God's divorce from Israel was prophesied by the Prophet Isaiah (50:1); nationally they are *"Lo-Ammi"* – not His people (Hosea 1:9). Israel fell and lost her divine favored-nation status, being temporarily cast away and scattered.

In God's current dispensation of grace, *"the middle wall of partition"* between Jews and the other nations has been broken down (Ephesians 2:14). There is now, therefore, before God, *"no difference between the Jew and the Greek"* (Romans 10:12), as *"God has concluded them all* [all nations *including* Israel] *in unbelief that He might have mercy on all"* (Romans 11:32) and believers of Jewish and other national descent are now being *"reconciled ... to God in one body by the cross"* (Ephesians 2:16).

National vanity now extends even to the modern-day state of "Israel." Zionism is the "Jewish" practice of nationalism without God, involving the restoration and support of a so-called "Jewish State."[1] There is *no* spiritual difference between Zionism and the godless nationalism of *any* other nation; but, sadly, many Christians are ignorant of this truth. One does not have to look far to find Christians supporting Zionism.

> There can be no kingdom without a king; therefore, while He is away, the kingdom must be in abeyance.
>
> — E.W. Bullinger

It is not uncommon to see the display of the Israeli flag as some "spiritual" act, or even its display side-by-side with the so-called "Christian flag." Some Christians actively support Israel, even giving monetarily for the return of Jews to Palestine.

These words should not be construed as anti-Semitic (a prejudice against or hostility towards Jewish people). Neither the Jews, nor their national state, are intrinsically *inferior* to that

---

1.   It will be God Himself Who will gather Abraham's descendants back to the land of Palestine; restore them as a righteous nation before Him; purging their sins; putting His Spirit and law in them, causing them to walk in His statutes, etc. (Jeremiah 31:33; 32:37; Ezekiel 11:17-18; 20:38; 36:24-29; Hebrews 8:10, 12; 10:16-17).

   Any premature work is simply the vanity of man. It must also be noted that when the coming *"Day of the Lord"* commences we will find that there are those already in place *"who say that they are Jews, and are not, and do lie"* (Revelation 2:9; 3:9). The Scriptures call them the *"synagogue of Satan."*

   The *"synagogue"* had *no* divine basis of authority in the Old Testament. Jewish worship was centered around the Temple in Jerusalem. Thus, we never encounter a phrase such as the *"synagogue of God."* It was a man-made religious fabrication, born while in Babylon, that stole the identity of God's work in Israel, similar to the way the "churches" of our day have stolen the identity of the Body of Christ. The *"synagogue"* went from the *"synagogue of the Jews"* in the Book of Acts (14:1; 17:1, 10), to the *"synagogue of Satan"* by the time you get to the opening of the Book of Revelation (2:9; 3:9).

of any other nation; *but* neither are they *superior* to any other nation at this time. They have no special national privilege before God as they had before. Instead, we seek to view them right where God currently has them: where they are *not His people*, and there is "*no difference.*" For the time being, their fallen condition has made them simply one of the nations. Their national status temporarily has been reduced to that of *all* other nations.

Yet, make no mistake about it, God is *not* done with Israel. When God has completed His current work with the church, the Body of Christ, and when "*the times* [eras] *of the nations are complete,*" He Himself will restore His "*beloved*" (Romans 11:28) to her preeminent position as the "*head,*" and "*the nations shall come to her light, and kings to the brightness of her rising*" (Isaiah 60:3). What a glorious day that will be for God's plan with the earth. To be ignorant of this important truth is to be "*wise in your own conceits*" (Romans 11:25).

However, in the meantime Israel has been reduced to the vanity of the rest of the nations – which two thousand years of history clearly demonstrates. Support of national Israel has no more or less spiritual value than the support of national Barbados. Leave it to Christians to try to undo what God in His purpose has done. An understanding of the revelation given to Paul would save Christians from such vain zeal.

God is demonstrating the futility of human government now, and has shown us that it will get worse until it is headed up in the man of sin. Shall we join it only to be condemned with it? Shall we seek to rule when we know that it is about to call down God's direct indignation? No! Our realm is inherent in the heavens, out of which we are awaiting a Savior (Philippians 3:20).

A.E. Knoch (1874-1965)
Unsearchable Riches
Volume 38, 1945, pages 8, 9

Chapter 5

Resident Aliens

Our citizenship is in heaven (Philippians 3:20, *KJV* margin).

Our commonwealth has its existence in the heavens (*Darby Translation*, 1890).

THE BELIEVER'S PAST

*W*hen we were born into this world, we were identified with Adam and all that his disobedience produced. We were a part of this *"present evil age"* (Galatians 1:4). We *"were in bondage under the elements of the world"* (Galatians 4:3). We walked *"according to the course of this world"* (Ephesians 2:2). In other words, we were earthly nationals; but the key word here is *were!*

*You **were** a part of the nations* (I Corinthians 12:2).

*You being **in the past** a part of the nations* (Ephesians 2:11).

THE BELIEVER'S PRESENT

God placed us into Christ, *"by Whom the world is crucified to"* us, and we *"to the world"* (Galatians 6:14). We are new crea-tures, *"old things are passed away; behold, all things are become new"* (II Corinthians 5:17). We are saints, delivered *"from the jurisdiction of dark-ness,"* and have been

> Our realm is inherent in the heavens, out of which we are awaiting a Savior.
>
> — Philippians 3:20

"transported into the kingdom of His dear Son" (Colossians 1:13). He *"has raised us up together, and made us sit together in heavenly places in Christ Jesus"* (Ephesians 2:6).

KINGDOMS IN CONFLICT

Being now a part of the celestial kingdom, we are thrust into a conflict of kingdoms. The kingdoms of this world, although ordained of God and carrying out His purpose, are currently in relative rebellion against the God of heaven. Yet He has given *us* a new and different calling, a glorious vocation, as ambassadors for Him and His kingdom; our function is now to shine as lights *"in the midst of a crooked and perverse na-tion"* (Philippians 2:15). We are now awaiting the *"fullness of the Nations"* (Romans 11:25).

It is easy to get caught up in the crosscurrents of national politics, for truly *"the heathen rage, and the people imagine a vain thing"* (Psalm 2:1; Acts 4:25). God, however, has trans-ferred us out of nationalism. The believer's home and citizen-ship are now in heaven.

With thanksgiving we can embrace the fact that we have been divinely *"transported"* from the *vain* kingdoms of this world into the glorious, celestial kingdom of His dear Son (Colossians 1:13). Thus, we are *"fellow-citizens with the saints"* (Ephesians 2:19) – foreigners here, citizens of the high-realm there. This world is not our homeland, as we are citizens of the commonwealth of heaven.

Regarding Philippians 3:20, J.C. O'Hair (1876-1958) wrote,

> The citizenship and politics of every representative of Christ is in heaven ... The believer is in the world, but not of the world. Unto him has been committed the Word of reconciliation. To him is given the ministry of reconciliation.[1]

Bill Petri also adds his voice to this discussion:

> The word *"conversation"* in Philippians 3:20 is an interesting word. It is the Greek word *politeuma* and means "the commonwealth of citizens." It is interesting that in the English language we take our word *politic* from this Greek word.[2]

> The citizenship and politics of every representative of Christ Is In heaven.
> — J.C. O'Hair

David C. Pack also shares the meaning of the word *politeuma* and its application to Paul's use of the phrase *"Body of Christ"*:

> The Greek word for citizenship is *politeuma*. "Politics" comes from this word! Christians *do* have a "political agenda," but it is not of *this* world.[3]

---

1. J.C. O'Hair, *Ambassadors of Reconciliation*.
2. William (Bill) Petri, *Government, War, and the Christian* (2008), p. 11.
3. David C. Pack, *Do Christians Vote?*

Dan Haden observes,

> A Greek city-state was known as a "polis." The original meaning was close to the idea of "town," but eventually was used to describe the ruling political center of a district or territory. In fact, *polis* became a rather complex word to encompass the whole idea of government, and was therefore a more extensive word than merely "town" or "city." We get the word *politics* from this word – the art or science of governing a group of people.

> Your interest in politics is genuine and God-given. Your actions are premature. Your realm is inherent in the heavens.

A politician is a person engaged in running the affairs of the *polis;* a policy is a reflection of wisdom in governing the *polis;* and police are those who control and regulate the activities of the *polis.* As you can see, this Greek word is foundational to many of our English words related to governmental matters.

In like fashion the Greek word *polis* was used by the Greeks as a basis for many other Greek words related to governmental functions. A *politarchēs* was a civil-magistrate (Acts 17:6, 8); a *politēs* was a citizen of the state (Acts 21:39); *politeia* was the word used for citizenship (Acts 22:28); and *politeuomai* was a word to describe how people were to conduct themselves as citizens of the state. Then there was the word we are considering here, *politeuma* – a word used to describe the state itself or a commonwealth. [4]

Paul teaches us that, as members of Christ's Body we already

---

4. Dan Haden, *Truth in Grace.*

have a citizenship, and it is in heaven. Our government is there; our King is there; our politics are there. We do not *belong* to an earthly kingdom; ours is a heavenly one.

Though we submit to them, earthly rulers are not ours; Christ is our King and only Potentate.

> *Our Lord Jesus Christ … Who is the blessed and only Potentate, the King of kings, and Lord of lords* (I Timothy 6:14-15).

This celestial kingdom is our *calling:*

> *Walk worthy of God, Who has called you to His kingdom and glory* (I Thessalonians 2:12).

We have been delivered from the earthly kingdoms and translated into His:

Who has delivered us from the power of darkness, and has translated us into the kingdom of His dear Son (Colossians 1:13).

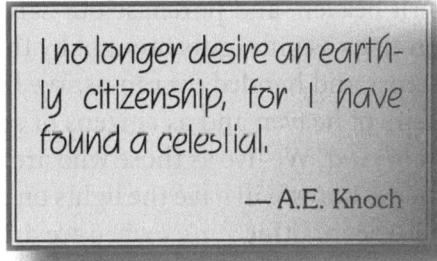

I no longer desire an earthly citizenship, for I have found a celestial.

— A.E. Knoch

He is our *only* Potentate (*"only Ruler"* Darby Translation, 1890), the King of kings, and Lord of lords:

> *Our Lord Jesus Christ: Who in His times He shall show, Who is the blessed and only Potentate, the King of kings, and Lord of lords* (I Timothy 6:14-15).

Lloyd Hartzler states that,

As an alien living in a foreign land is disqualified from taking part in politics, so the heavenly citizen disqualifies himself in view of his higher allegiance.[5]

What follows is a collection of quotations about our true citizenship.

CITIZENS OF HEAVEN

> We are not earthly people having heavenly experiences; we are heavenly people having earthly experiences.
>
> — Martin Zender

We are not citizens of this world trying to make our way to heaven; we are citizens of heaven trying to make our way through this world. That radical Christian insight can be life-changing. We are not to live so as to earn God's love, inherit heaven, and purchase our salvation. All of those are given to us as gifts; gifts brought by the Lord Jesus Christ on the cross and handed over to us. We live as God's redeemed, as heirs of heaven and as citizens of another land: the Kingdom of God. We live as those who are on a journey home – a home we know will have the lights on and the door open and our Father waiting for us when we arrive. That means in all adversity our worship of God is joyful, our life is hopeful, our future is secure. There is nothing we can lose on earth that can rob us of the treasures God has given us and will give us.

The Landisfarne Magazine

WE'RE CITIZENS OF HEAVEN

We are in this world, but we do not belong here. We are only

---

5. Lloyd Hartzler, *The Christian and the State*, p. 6.

strangers, pilgrims. We travel abroad. We visit cities, looking upon beautiful things, charmed by what we see, but we are only tourists. Something tugs at our hearts continually – it is home. So while we still live in this world we are citizens of heaven. Christ is our King (I Timothy 1:17). We owe him our allegiance, our obedience. We are to seek those things which are above, where Christ is.

J.R. Miller (1840-1912)
The Wider Life (1908)

THE AGENDA OF THE KINGDOM OF GOD

The church that belongs to Jesus is not part of anyone's agenda. In fact, people who belong to Him provide the only agenda that ultimately counts. It is the agenda of the Kingdom of God breaking into human history – the central feature in the history of the world. It is the only force that can make an enemy into a friend, a criminal into a saint, a biological father into a real parent. And it makes the most ambitious political agenda we can possibly imagine look trivial by comparison.

> I no longer desire an earthly citizenship, for I have found a celestial.
>
> — A.E. Knoch

Cal Thomas (with Ed Dobson)
Blinded by Might: Can the Religious Right Save America?
(1999), page 97

OUR ALLEGIANCE

Scripture teaches that we are to view ourselves as soldiers stationed in a foreign country, and thus are not to let ourselves get overly entangled in civilian affairs [*"the affairs of this life"* II

Timothy 2:4]. Whatever country we may naturally belong to, Paul says we are to remember always that our real citizenship is in heaven (*cf.* Philippians 3:20). Whatever opinions we have about how to solve society's problems, we are to remember always that we cannot serve two masters (Luke 16:13).

Our allegiance, therefore, can never be to any version of the kingdom-of-the-world, however much better we may think it is than other versions of the kingdom-of-the-world. Our allegiance is to our heavenly Father, whose country we belong to and into whose family we've been adopted (Romans 8:29; Galatians 1:2; 6:10; Ephesians 1:4-5) ... We are to see ourselves as "alien residents."

Gregory A. Boyd
The Myth of a Christian Nation (2005), page 70, 71

FRIENDLY ALIENS IN A FOREIGN LAND

The Christian is called to be a pilgrim and a stranger. He must suffer quietly the present discomforts and risks of being out of gear with the world's mighty machinery, national and international.

Christ's follower is to *"set"* his *"affection on things above, not on things on the earth"* (Colossians 3:2). No one can be both a pilgrim passing through a given country *and* a citizen of it. In relation to this present world system we cheerfully adopt the former status. To the end of his sojourn the right-minded alien, wherever he may be, will do his utmost to benefit those about him; but his activities must be conducted by his alienship.

The heart of an alien should be set on the things of his fatherland, where are his sovereign, his home and his permanent estates, and should not be "set" on the land where he is only a stranger and sojourner. Now an ambassador is never a citizen of any state save that which sends him.

G.H. Lang (1874-1958)
The Christian a Friendly Alien

Do Good to All[6]

As we have therefore opportunity, let us do good unto all men (Galatians 6:10).

Instead of crusading and picketing against all of the perceived evils in our culture, believers would better glorify Christ by manifesting kindness and love.

Instead of complaining about our government's tendency to waste money on useless programs, believers should open their hearts and their purses to care for those in need.

Instead of blocking the doors (or worse) to abortion clinics, they should open the doors of their homes to pregnant women who don't need a "Pro-life" lecture, but loving acceptance and assistance in carrying their babies to term.

These are but a few of the practical ways believers can demonstrate the love of Christ instead of becoming objects of ridicule by constantly engaging in all of the negative rhetoric about how bad our society is.

Lost Distinctive

To a large degree, we've lost our distinct kingdom-of-God vision and abandoned our mission. We've allowed the world to define us, set our agenda, and define the terms of our en-

6. This section, "Do Good to All," is taken from *Bible Students Notebook #223*, adapted from the writings of Jon Zens and Cliff Bjork, *God and Country: The Dangers of Contemporary Christian Americanism.*

gagement with it. We've accepted the limited and divisive kingdom-of-the-world options and therefore mirror the kingdom-of-the-world conflicts.

Gregory A. Boyd
The Myth of a Christian Nation, page 64

Remember your high calling. You are an ambassador of Christ – you are entrusted with the most honorable and important vocation that can engage and animate the heart of man!

John Newton (1725-1807)
Author of the Hymn, *Amazing Grace*
John Newton's Letters
July 13, 1776

Chapter 6

Celestial Ambassadors

We are ambassadors for Christ (II Corinthians 5:20).

As believers, not only is our citizenship in heaven, but we also have the high honor of functioning as representatives of our celestial homeland here on earth. We are celestial ambassadors.

Our ambassadorship is a truly neglected area. A few other authors share with us some observations on ambassadorship as it relates to our divine commission.

> Where is the King today? He is in heaven, a Royal Exile, unwanted by the world. And where is the kingdom today? That too, like many a government since, is in exile. It is vested in the King Himself. It remains in heaven while its earthly establishment is held in abeyance. And where is the believer's spiritual citizenship today? In heaven!
>
> Why then are we left here? To represent Christ – and the very title Christ means "the Anointed One," the King.
>
> *We are ambassadors for Christ* (II Corinthians 5:20).

To better understand our position as ambassadors for Christ, let us consider the position of ambassadorship itself.

1. An ambassador is an official representative of a ruler or state. It would do us all good to realize anew that God has us here to represent His Son.

2. An ambassador is always sent to another nation, never to his own. It may at first seem unnecessary to point this out, but it is most important here; for the fact that our Lord is sending ambassadors to all the world implies that He has no nation on earth which He calls His Own.

   We speak of Christian nations, but in reality there is not one single government on the earth of which it can possibly be said, "This is the kingdom of God. Christ reigns here." Israel was once on their way to becoming the kingdom of God, but she refused the King from heaven and the kingdom of heaven and has been cast out of God's favor until *"the day of His power"* when He will make her *"willing"* (Psalm 110:3).

3. An exchange of ambassadors denotes a state of peace.

4. Ambassadors are withdrawn when war is declared.

Cornelius R. Stam (1909-2003)
Ambassadors for Christ

An ambassador has no part in the government of the land in which he serves, but rather represents his own country that sent him, seeking its best interests. Are we, then, any less truly foreigners here because it is heaven that is the land of our citizenship (Philippians 3:20), and the saints are our fellow-citizens? (Ephesians 2:19).

If, then, we refuse to mingle in politics, it is not that we think politics in itself is wrong, but that we belong to another country, that is, a heavenly; and we see that the world [system] is evil (John 17:15), and rejects the One we love. We wish to be separate from it therefore, and to cast in our lot with Him. We are drawn upward, above and beyond this scene, by union with Christ on high; willing to be despised, yea, rather to suffer shame for His name, while we wait for Him to come.

E.V.W.
Help and Food (1912)[1]

Our relation to the governments of the earth is clearly defined by one word. We are *ambassadors*. Sent from the court of heaven, we represent the divine government on the earth so long as the peace which the conciliation brings may last. Before God declares war with the earth, we, as His ambassadors, will be withdrawn. In the meanwhile it should be our settled policy to conciliate. The ambassador's business has to do only with peace. His work ends when war is declared. So we should use every effort to be at peace with the governments with which we come in contact, relying on God to restrain them from forcing us to do that which is displeasing to Him. He will see to it that a frank, free confession of our faith will receive consideration at the hands of the powers that be, which, as we have said, are *His* ministers, working out His purpose, even though they may not be aware of it. We stand for peace, not merely with other nations, but also with the government under which we live.

Unsearchable Riches
Volume 10 (1918)

---

1. Cited in *Can Consistent Christians Mingle in Politics?* Published by *Moments With the Book*

We are called to be ambassadors for our heavenly government to these present earthly governments. The word *"conversation"* in Philippians 3:20 is an interesting word. It is the Greek word "politeuma" and means "the commonwealth of citizens." It is interesting that in the English language we take our word *politic* from this Greek word. The political language used here, to be sure, is no coincidence … The Body of Christ has its *"conversation* [citizenship] *in heaven."* As citizens of heaven, while on earth, we serve as Christ's ambassadors.

Paul's use of the term *"ambassador"* to describe the role of believers was an excellent choice. We live under a foreign government – the human governments which are controlled by Satan. Just as earthly ambassadors do not take part in the governments they reside under, believers should not take part in earthly governments. Instead, recognizing that our citizenship lies in heaven, we should serve as representatives to those around us; we should serve as ambassadors for Christ.

William Petri
Government, War, and the Christian (2008), pages 11-13

ON ASSIGNMENT

We who have trusted Christ are citizens of heaven (Philippians 3:20; *KJV* margin, *Darby, Young*). We are here on foreign soil – "on assignment." If we were in our own country we would not be subject to any of the cares and sorrows of this life; but as ambassadors to a world that is currently at enmity with God, we are constantly faced with the burdens of such a *divine* "appointment."

That no man should be moved by these afflictions: for

*yourselves know that **we are appointed thereto*** (I Thessalonians 3:3).

We are here to take our full share in the trials under which the *"whole creation groans and travails in pain together until now"* (Romans 8:22). Each of us is part of that of which Job spoke, *"Yet man is born to trouble, as the sparks fly upward"* (Job 5:7). We, in identity with Christ, suffer so that others may know of His wondrous and full grace. Next to our salvation we should have as our greatest desire that God would use us as His vessels of mercy. We suffer the perils of broken humanity *for His sake.*

> *As it is written, **"For Your sake** we are killed all the day long; we are accounted as sheep for the slaughter"* (Romans 8:36).

Each day that He extends free grace to mankind is but another day of extension to our "tour of duty," but He will "make it up to us."

> *Let us not be weary in well doing: for in due season we shall reap, if we faint not* (Galatians 6:9).

> *Therefore, my beloved brothers, be steadfast, unmovable, always abounding in the work of the Lord, forasmuch as you know that your labor is not in vain in the Lord* (I Corinthians 15:58).

As we find ourselves *"in infirmities, in reproaches, in necessities, in persecutions, in distresses for Christ's sake"* (II Corinthians 12:10), let's not forget that *"we are appointed thereto"* (I Thessalonians 3:3).

Be mindful of our *honored* appointment; we are on *divine assignment! We are celestial ambassadors.*

People say I have to know what's going on in the world. I say, "Show me the verse." It's fascinating, but no one has yet shown me the verse. If there was such a verse, I am convinced I would have been shown it by now.

Martin Zender
Clanging Gong News
Volume 1, No. 10
Bad News Blues

Chapter 7

Seek and Set
Those Things Which Are Above

If you then are risen with Christ, seek those things which are above, where Christ sits on the right hand of God. Set your affection on things above, not on things on the earth. For you are dead, and your life is hid with Christ in God. When Christ, Who is our life, shall appear, then shall you also appear with Him in glory (Colossians 3:1-4).

Paul tells us to do two things regarding *"those things which are above."* First he tells us to, *"seek"* them – there are some glorious *"things that are above"* for which we are to *"seek."* Then after we have found them, he tells us to *"set"* our affection on them.

Our English word "seek" has a meaning of,

To go in search or quest of; to look for; to search for by going from place to place.[1]

---

1. Noah Webster, *American Dictionary of the English Language*, 1828.

Its etymology means,

> To follow; for to seek is to go after, and the primary sense is to advance, to press, to drive forward.[2]

Our English word "*set*" has a meaning of,

> To put, place or fix in any situation.[3]

He builds too low who builds beneath the skies.

In the *King James Version*, the Greek word here translated "*set*" (*phroneo*) is also translated as *savor*,[4] *think*,[5] *mind*,[6] *regard*,[7] and *care*.[8]

Of course, Paul does not leave us in the dark concerning "*those things which are above.*" He has revealed them to us, planting them throughout his writings for us to "*seek.*" This is our purpose here: to identify from Paul's letters a few of "*those things which are above,*" so that we may follow the admonition of our apostle to "*seek*" and "*set.*" Five of these are right here in our "*seek and set*" passage (Colossians 3:1-4).

Christ

> "*Where **Christ** sits …*" (Colossians 3:1).

Our Lord Jesus Christ is to be the object of our seeking and setting. He is seated at the Right Hand of God. We will never

---

2. *Ibid.*
3. *Ibid.*
4. Matthew 16:23; Mark 8:33.
5. Acts 28:22; Romans 12:3; I Corinthians 4:6; Philippians 1:7.
6. Romans 8:5; 12:16; II Corinthians 13:11; Galatians 5:10; Philippians 2:2, 5; 3:15-16, 19; 4:2.
7. Romans 14:6.
8. Philippians 4:10.

exhaust the richness of His person and work. This was the passion of Paul, as his heart revealed itself to the Philippian saints.

> *What things were gain to me, those I counted loss for Christ. Yes, doubtless, and I count all things but loss for the excellency of the knowledge of Christ Jesus my Lord: for Whom I have suffered the loss of all things, and do count them but dung, that I may win Christ, and be found in Him, not having my own righteousness, which is of the law, but that which is through the faith of Christ, the righteousness which is of God by faith: That I may know Him, and the power of His resurrection, and the fellowship of His sufferings, being made conformable to His death* (Philippians 3:7-10).

The Right-Hand Throne

*"... on the **right-hand** ..."* (Colossians 3:1).

We are to seek for and set our affections on God's right-hand throne.

> Civilizing the world ... and acquiring earthly power and wealth - Such notions are founded on Israelitish Old Testament promises.
>
> — C.I. Scofield

Not only is the Lord Jesus Christ seated there, but this is the place of our present position and standing in Him as well as our future and final destiny with Him. Because we are the sons of God, we are His heirs as well; and, of course, the Lord Jesus Christ's joint-heirs. We are joint-possessors of all that Father possesses. We share these riches with our Savior and Head.

> *We are the children of God: and if children, then heirs; heirs of God, and joint-heirs with Christ* (Romans 8:16).

And has raised us up together, and made us sit together in heavenly places in Christ Jesus (Ephesians 2:6).

God

"*... of **God**"* (Colossians 3:1).

The God of the universe is to be the focus of our seeking and setting. He is not just the universe's Almighty: He is our loving and precious Father.

Grace be to you, and peace, from God our Father, and from the Lord Jesus Christ (Ephesians 1:2).

Because you are sons, God has sent forth the Spirit of His Son into your hearts, crying, "Abba, Father" (Galatians 4:6).

For you have not received the spirit of bondage again to fear; but you have received the Spirit of adoption, whereby we cry, "Abba, Father" (Romans 8:15).

Because our identity is in the Lord Jesus Christ, we now can speak the language of a son! The intimate term that our Lord Jesus Christ used for the Father was *"Abba."*

He said, "Abba, Father" (Mark 14:36).

Our Life

"*... your life is hid with Christ in God. When Christ, Who is **our life** ..."* (Colossians 3:3-4).

We are to seek for and set our affections on our *real* life. Christ is our life. We are alive with Divine life, through Him.

I am crucified with Christ: nevertheless I live; yet not I, but Christ lives in me: and the life which I now live in the flesh I live by the faith of the Son of God, Who loved me, and gave Himself for me (Galatians 2:20).

Glory

*"... appear with Him in **glory**"* (Colossians 3:4).

The final example that Paul gave us in this immediate passage of what we are to seek for and set our affections on is *"glory."* This, too, is our final destiny. We who had *"come short of the glory of God"* (Romans 3:23) will *"appear with Him in glory."*

By Whom also we have access by faith into this grace wherein we stand, and rejoice in hope of the glory of God (Romans 5:2).

So also is the resurrection of the dead. It is sown in corruption; it is raised in incorruption: It is sown in dishonor; it is raised in glory ... (I Corinthians 15:42-43).

Therefore I endure all things for the elect's sakes, that they may also obtain the salvation which is in Christ Jesus with eternal glory (II Timothy 2:10).

I calculate that the sufferings of this present time are not worthy to be compared with the glory which shall be revealed in us (Romans 8:18).

For our light affliction, which is but for a moment, works for us a far more exceeding weight of glory, lasting for the ages (II Corinthians 4:17).

That He might make known the riches of His glory on

the vessels of mercy, which He had before prepared to glory (Romans 9:23).

We speak the wisdom of God in a mystery, even the hidden wisdom, which God ordained before the world to our glory (I Corinthians 2:7).

The eyes of your understanding being enlightened; that you may know what is the hope of His calling, and what are the riches of the glory of His inheritance in the saints (Ephesians 1:18).

To whom God would make known what is the riches of the glory of this mystery among the nations; which is Christ in you, the hope of glory (Colossians 1:27).

That you would walk worthy of God, Who has called you to His kingdom and glory (I Thessalonians 2:12).

Whereto He called you by our gospel, to the obtaining of the glory of our Lord Jesus Christ (II Thessalonians 2:14).

Do not be distracted from what is *real* by the make-believe of this world – its system and course. Instead, diligently *"seek"* the *"things that are above," "setting"* your affection on them, for we have *"the high calling of God in Christ Jesus."*

Nations are not given in order that we may have good government. Nations are a part of God's program in order to demonstrate the inability of man to govern without Him.

A.E. Knoch (1874-1965)
Unsearchable Riches
Volume 36, 1945

Chapter 8

Paul and His Roman Citizenship

Is it lawful for you to scourge a man who is a Roman, and uncondemned? (A.D. 58; Acts 22:25).

Some believe that passages such as this from the *Book of Acts* somehow show that Paul was advocating active involvement in nationalism. However, things are not always as they *first* appear.

THE NATURE OF THE *BOOK OF ACTS*

One must be careful about establishing their doctrine from the *Book of Acts*. This book was not written by Paul, nor was it written to establish doctrine for the Body of Christ, nor was it designed to be a pattern for our practical living. Instead, *Acts* is a book that reveals the transitional history of the fall of Israel and the rise of the Body of Christ. Therefore, to obtain truth for the church, the Body of Christ, one must turn to the epistles of Paul.

WHAT PAUL WAS *NOT* DOING

Paul did, on occasion appeal to Roman law; but this can't remotely be compared with being an active participant in influencing and determining governmental policy. Neither Paul nor Jesus ever tried to reform Caesar or the Roman government.

WHAT PAUL *WAS* DOING

To understand what Paul was doing when appealing to Roman law, we need the historical background to understand the passages where Paul brings up the issue of citizenship (A.D. 59; Acts 22-25).

First, let's realize that all throughout Paul's earlier 20-year apostolic ministry as recorded in the *Book of Acts,* he is never recorded as having made any such reference to citizenship, even in the face of severe torture. A Roman citizen was protected from such treatment, nevertheless without any apparent appeal from him he received 39 stripes on five different occasions, and was three times beaten with rods (all prior to A.D. 57; II Corinthians 11:24). So why does he suddenly change and make an appeal?

The background of events will provide us with the answer. Paul had for *"many years"* (Romans 15:23) desired to make a trip to Rome; but he had been *"much hindered"* (Romans 15:22) because of constant delays caused by persecution from unbelieving Jews. Paul planned to make a trip to Jerusalem to deliver relief that he had been raising for the poor saints there. His plan was then to move on to Rome after that, provided that he is *"delivered from them that do not believe in Judaea"* (Romans 15:31).

After these things were ended, Paul purposed in the spir-

*it, when he had passed through Macedonia and Achaia, to go to Jerusalem, saying, "After I have been there, **I must also see Rome**"* (Spring, A.D. 54; Acts 19:21).

Paul wrote to the saints at Rome to inform them of his plans to come to them.

For I long to see you [the saints in Rome], *that I may impart to you some spiritual gift, to the end you may be established. ... I have been much hindered from coming to you; but now having no more place in these parts, and having a great desire these many years to come to you, when I take my journey into Spain, I will come to you: for I trust to see you in my journey ... But now I go to Jerusalem to minister to the saints. ... When I have performed this, and have sealed to them this fruit, I will come ... I am sure that, when I come to you, I shall come in the fullness of the blessing of the gospel of Christ. ... That I may be delivered from them who do not believe in Judaea; and that my service which I have for Jerusalem may be accepted of the saints; that I may come to you with joy by the will of God, and may with you be refreshed* (Spring, A.D. 58; Romans 1:11; 15:22-32).

While at Jerusalem heavy opposition broke out against him. Seizing on an opportunity to be delivered from the unbelieving Jews so that he could finally take his ministry to the capitol of the Roman Empire, he simply inquired, *"Is it lawful for you to scourge a man that is a Roman, and uncondemned?"* (Acts 22:25).

Paul appealed for the civil authorities to act in accordance with the law which bound THEM. He appealed to the principle of Roman law, an intervention that delivered him from the hands of the Jewish persecution. With his opposition constrained, Paul now only needed a means to get to Rome.

He saw this opportunity in exercising Roman rights to *"appeal* [his case] *to Caesar"* (A.D. 59; Acts 25:11). The government saw Paul as a Roman citizen, and Paul *related* to their treatment of him as such – pressing on them the standard of **their** *own law* – and as a result he was able to make his long-desired trip to Rome under Roman authority.

A GREATER REVELATION

Now, before we assume that statements found in the *Book of Acts* have some instruction for the believer to become political, we must first be careful not to anticipate revelation. This is a significant concern when reading the Scriptures. We need to recognize that Paul received an abundance of *progressive* revelations over his some thirty-year apostleship.

> *I* **will** **come** *to visions and revelations of the Lord ... through the abundance of the revelations* (Autumn, A.D. 57; II Corinthians 12:1, 7).

It must be remembered that, even *if* Paul intended to *advocate* an earthly citizenship in the *Book of Acts,* later, on receiving greater revelation from the Lord, he clarified the issue entirely. While in a Roman prison God gave him additional revelation which he recorded in his letter to the Philippians. This was a revelation of singleness of mind, and a Roman prison was quite an amazing place for such a celestial revelation.

> **OUR CITIZENSHIP IS IN HEAVEN;** *from where also we look for the Savior, the Lord Jesus Christ* (A.D. 62; Philippians 3:20).

Paul did not write, *"one of our citizenships is in heaven,"* or *"we have another citizenship in heaven,"* or *"we have two citizenships, one of which is in heaven."* Instead he writes *abso-*

lutely and plainly of one SINGULAR *"citizenship."* From his Roman bondage he boldly and without qualification declares this citizenship to be **celestial.**

We are called to the ministry of conciliation and must not oppose those whom God has been pleased to put over us in any matter which does not violate our conscience.

Unsearchable Riches
Volume 10, 1918

Chapter 9

Paul and Nationalism

Be followers of me, even as I also am of Christ (I Corinthians 11:1).

Be followers of me (I Corinthians 4:16).

Be followers together of me (Philippians 3:17).

EXAMPLES FROM PAUL

Appeal for Equity

As we noticed in the last chapter, in the Book of Acts there is an account in the life of Paul that leaves us an example in appealing to the nations for equity.

As they bound him with thongs, Paul said to the centurion that stood by, "Is it lawful for you to whip a man who is a Roman, and uncondemned?" (Acts 22:25).

When Paul had appealed to be reserved to the hearing of Augustus, I commanded him to be kept until I might send him to Caesar (Acts 25:21).

Making such an appeal has a testimony on the conscience of the unbelievers, regardless of their resulting actions and decrees – even if ultimately they seem unjust. Paul's appeals brought the government officials face to face with the gospel as well as with their own accountability to the divine authority which they used.

> We may appeal to civil government, especially where scriptural principle is involved or the recognition of faith refused, or in any matter which would hinder the work of the kingdom of God. We may appeal for due treatment under the law.[1]

Reporting Dangers

Another account from the life of Paul, as found in the Book of Acts – the reporting of dangerous situations for governmental restraint.

> *When Paul's nephew heard of their lying in wait, he went and entered into the castle, and told Paul. Then Paul called one of the centurions to him, and said, "Bring this young man to the chief captain: far he has a certain thing to tell him." So he took him, and brought him to the chief captain, and said, "Paul the prisoner called me to him, and prayed me to bring this young man to you, who has something to say to you." Then the chief captain took him by the hand, and went with him aside privately and asked him, "What do you have to tell me?" And he said, "The Jews have agreed to desire you that you would bring down Paul tomorrow into the council, as though they would inquire somewhat of him more perfectly. But don't yield to them: for there lie in wait for him of them more than forty men, which have bound themselves with an oath, that they will neither*

---

1.   Lloyd Hartzler, *The Christian and the State*, p. 17.

eat nor drink until they have killed him: and now are they ready, looking for a promise from you." So the chief captain then let the young man depart, and charged him, "See that you tell no man that you have shown these things to me" (Acts 23:16-22).

Paul's example could be used as a precedent for us to call the police, or other appropriate authorities, if we saw a prowler in our backyard, or if we witnessed some injustice being committed.

INSTRUCTIONS FROM PAUL

Settling Differences Between Believers

On the other hand, Paul tells us *not* to turn to the national judicial system of unbelievers in solving conflicts with other believers.

How dare any of you, having a matter against another, go to law before the unjust, and not before the saints? Don't you know that the saints will judge the world? And if the world will be judged by you, are you unworthy to judge the smallest matters? Don't you know that we shall judge angels? How much more things that pertain to this life? If then you have judgments of things pertaining to this life, set them to judge who are least esteemed in the church. I speak to your shame. Is it so, that there is not a wise man among you? No, not one who shall be able to judge between his brothers? But brother goes to law with brother,

> The era of the Gentiles has a purpose which is the opposite of that of the Kingdom of God.
>
> — A.E. Knoch

and that before unbelievers. Now therefore there is ut-
terly a fault among you, because you go to law one with
another. Why do you not rather take wrong? Why do
you not rather suffer yourselves to be defrauded? No,
you do wrong, and defraud, and that your brothers (I
Corinthians 6:1-8).

Evil in the World

Paul also clearly instructs us of our attitude and response to
all of the evil of the world.

See that no one renders evil for evil to any man; but ever
follow that which is good, both among yourselves, and to
all men (I Thessalonians 5:15).

Return to no one evil for evil. Display nobility before all
men. If possible, as much as lies in you, cultivate peace
with all mankind. Dearly beloved, don't retaliate, but
recede from the place of anger: for it is written, "Vin-
dication[2] belongs to Me;[3] I will make it up to you," says
the Lord. Therefore if your enemy hungers, feed him; if
he thirsts, give him drink: for in so doing you will heap
coals of fire on his head.[4] Don't be conquered by evil, but
conquer evil with good (Romans 12:17-21).

Praying and Giving Thanks

Last but not least, Paul instructs us to pray and give thanks
for *"all who are in authority."*

I exhort therefore, that, first of all, supplications,
prayers, intercessions and giving of thanks be made for

---

2. "Vindication" belongs only to the God of love.

3. Divine "vindication" is about setting right the wrongs, by "repaying,"
"recompensing" or "restoring" what has been lost through injustice.

4. See Appendix 1: *Heaping Coals of Fire.*

all men; for kings, and for all who are in authority; that
we may lead a quiet and peaceable life in all godliness
and honesty (I Timothy 2:1-2).

SIDETRACKED

When our attention is diverted from Christ and focused on
man with all of his perpetual governmental corruptions, we
are sidetracked from our present purpose and function on
earth.

Finally, brothers, whatever things are true, whatever
things are honest, whatever things are just, whatever
things are pure, whatever things are lovely, whatever
things are of good report; if there is any virtue, and if
there is any praise, think on these things (Philippians
4:8).

For to be carnally minded is death; but to be spiritually
minded is life and peace (Romans 8:6).

Hardly *any* thoughts related to *any* earthly government
could be described as true, honest, just, pure, lovely or of a
good report.

Many, with good intentions, would have the believer become
well informed concerning the evils and vices of government
and society. Paul, on the other hand, entreats the believer to be

Wise to that which is good, and simple concerning evil[5]
(Romans 16:19).

The conservative "Evangelical Christian" activists will go to
great lengths for the shock-treatment of information regarding the ills of nationalism (*i.e.,* the Gentiles, the heathen):

---

5. *"I want you to be experts in good and innocents in evil"* (Moffatt).

"Look!" "Can you believe it?" "What a shame and disgrace!"
"How shocking?" While, once again, our apostle pleads,

> *It is a shame even to speak of those things which are
> done of them in secret* (Ephesians 5:12).

THE BELIEVER'S RESPONSIBILITIES

Mr. Hartzler has some interesting comments regarding the
believer's responsibilities toward nationalism, by showing
what they are *not*.

Not Identification: Jesus told Pilate, *"My kingdom is not of this
world ... now is my kingdom not from hence."* If Jesus' kingdom was presently of this world, His children would take an
active part – *"then would my servants fight"* (John 18:36).

Not Reformation: Some people feel strongly that the
Christian should help elect better men, clean up politics,
vote out evil, and help put a Christian into office. From
the moralist's viewpoint this sounds good. How does this
square with the New Testament Scriptures?

The church has a higher calling than to affect these condi-
tions by election. Voting "good" men into office will never
put sin away from the heart of men. *"He [Jesus] appeared
to put away sin by the sacrifice of Himself"* (Hebrews 9:26).
In the New Testament days the apostles did not put on a
campaign to abolish slavery. Neither did they try to clean
up Roman politics and straighten out civil injustices. This
is not the church's approach to the issues, neither will it
solve the problems. Only the power of the Gospel will
penetrate to the root of man's need. If the church becomes
involved in community or national reformation attempts,
it will lose its power.[6]

---

6. Lloyd Hartzler, *The Christian and the State*, p. 5, 6.

THE BELIEVER'S SOURCE OF LIBERTY

The believer's source of freedom does not come from any "freedom fighter," or from any nation. Paul plainly tells us *our* source of liberty:

> *Now the Lord is that Spirit: and where the Spirit of the Lord is, there is liberty* (II Corinthians 3:17).

No matter what our circumstances, we are always *free*.

> *He who is called in the Lord, being a servant* [in bondage], *is the Lord's freeman* (I Corinthians 7:22).

Spiritually, believers are the *only real* freemen; all others are in bondage! The "land of the free" is where we are seated in Christ in the celestials. This is *"the high calling of God in Christ Jesus."*

The government of the United States is not, in any sense, founded on the Christian religion.

John Adams (1735-1826)
Treaty of Tripoli
1796

Tucked away in our national mythology is the notion that America is a redeemer nation.

Donald B. Kraybill
Our Star-Spangled Faith
1976

This, we are told, is a Christian nation. This is very hard to realize. What is a Christian? He loves his enemies. That is one of the real tests. He does good to them that persecute him. Is this the charter under which the nation operates? But when Christ comes, then we will see these things carried out. There will be government that is Christlike, and in accord with God's will.

A.E. Knoch (1874-1965)
Unsearchable Riches
Volume 36, 1945

Chapter 10

Is the United States a Christian Nation?

Over the past two decades, as the truth of our *"high calling of God in Christ Jesus"* was pressed on my heart, I began an active search for others who may have written regarding this truth in its relationship to nationalism. The next few chapters are mainly compilations of excerpts from various authors that I located. Although only a handful of these are from sources that we wholeheartedly endorse, they are nonetheless quite amazing testimonies to truth.

The Myth of a Christian Nation

I believe that a significant segment of American evangelicalism is guilty of nationalistic and political idolatry. To a frightful degree, I think, evangelicals fuse the kingdom of God with a preferred version of the kingdom of the world.

What gives the connection between Christianity and politics such strong emotional force in the U.S.? I believe it is the longstanding myth that America is a Christian nation.

Throughout our history, most Americans have assumed our nation's causes and wars were righteous and just, and that "God is on our side." In our minds – as so often in our sanctuaries – the cross and the American flag stand side by side. Our allegiance to God tends to go hand in hand with our allegiance to country. Consequently, many Christians who take their faith seriously see themselves as the religious guardians of a Christian homeland. America, they believe, is a holy city "set on a hill," and the church's job is to keep it shining.

For many in America and around the world, the American flag has smothered the glory of the cross, and the ugliness of our American version of Caesar has squelched the radiant love of Christ. Because the myth that America is a Christian nation has led many to associate America with Christ, many now hear the good news of Jesus only as American news, capitalistic news, imperialistic news, exploitive news, antigay news, or Republican news. Whether justified or not, many people want nothing to do with any of it.

Gregory A. Boyd
The Myth of a Christian Nation (2005), pages 11-13

THE REDEEMER NATION

While listening to the news I heard a Presidential candidate refer to the United States as "the hope of the world."

Donald B. Kraybill addresses this mindset in his book, Our Star-Spangled Faith:

> Tucked away in our national mythology is the notion that America is a redeemer nation. We are led to believe that

the American Messiah brings salvation to the rest of the world. The American way of life redeems the cultures of other countries. God will use the American nation to magnify Himself among other nations.

Donald B. Kraybill
Our Star-Spangled Faith (1976, Herald Press), pages 18, 43

NATIONAL IDOLATRY

America's "God and Country" priests love places of honor at Presidential prayer breakfasts, football games, parades and political conventions. America places pious phrases in public places ("In God We Trust") and wraps the good news of salvation through Jesus Christ in the stars and stripes, leading her citizens into a kind of national idolatry.

Jesus is not partial to the United States. He loves the whole world.

Donald B. Kraybill
Our Star-Spangled Faith (1976, Herald Press), back cover

"GOD AND COUNTRY" PROPAGANDA

How far does this "God and Country" propaganda run? Listen to what a past president of the *National Council for the Encouragement of Patriotism* has to say:

When I place my right hand over my heart as that glorious American flag passes by, I feel very near to God.

Newsweek
June 15, 1970, page 30

A Nationalized Gospel[1]

A very vocal element within mainstream Christianity promotes a *nationalized gospel* – a gospel wrapped in an American flag. Unbiblical notions about patriotism and America's "special" place in God's plan abound in books, magazines, radio and TV programs produced by these religio-political zealots, as well as from their pulpits.

To equate nationalism, American or any other, with faithfulness to the gospel is a misguided perspective that can only serve to weaken our witness to the saving grace of God through Jesus Christ. When such nationalistic battle cries dominate our agendas, the true message of the gospel will be inevitably compromised, if not forgotten altogether. It is time for us to "test the spirits" that are urging us to "turn America back to God and traditional 'Judeo-Christian' values."

Christ did not call us to reform our *country*, but to spread the *only* message that has the power to change *lives*. If we truly believe in the power of the gospel, we must not let it be weighed down by such unbiblical baggage.

It Goes Like This …

The proposition that America *as a nation* occupies a special place in God's earthly purpose (with the implication that America is better than other nations) is generally based on arguments much like those expounded in the following excerpt:

---

1. This section is the first of seven of this chapter that are taken from *Bible Students Notebook* #223, adapted from the writings of Jon Zens and Cliff Bjork, *God and Country: The Dangers of Contemporary Christian Americanism.* The sections include: "A Nationalized Gospel," "Is Any Nation 'Better' than Another," "Who Really Places Presidents and Kings in Power," "The Success of the Gospel," "Traditional Values," "To Which Political Party Does God Belong," and "Our Confidence."

The United States is a blessed nation, founded on Godly principles by devout God-fearing men and women. From the personal writings of the authors of our constitution, we learn that they looked to God for the wisdom to guide our country's affairs. God has a blueprint for keeping our country great and it's found in II Chronicles 7:14.

This is typical of the kind of reasoning that is common to most of the advocates of such agendas. The problem is that it is based on alleged facts that simply are not true. It is repeatedly maintained, for example, that God's blessing upon America as a nation has its roots in the "godly" perspectives and objectives of its founding fathers. To make such an assertion demonstrates either a complete ignorance of America's early history or, worse yet, an act of deliberate revisionism.

Is Any Nation "Better" than Another?

The notion that America has been blessed more than other nations because of her alleged "godly" beginning is not only without foundation, but it has spawned other errant teaching as well. Building on that false premise, we are told that the divine "blessing" America has enjoyed will be replaced by "judgment" if Christians do not do their part to bring about a *national* moral reform. God measures nations by their adherence to the Ten Commandments, we are told, and blesses or curses accordingly.

> *Blessed is the nation whose God is the Lord; and the people whom He hath chosen for His own inheritance* (Psalm 33:12).

To apply Psalm 33:12 to the United States is totally inappropriate. It is typical of interpretation that fails to take Paul's revelation into consideration before making such an application. Prior to the gospel of the grace of God, the nation of Israel alone was the undeserving, yet divinely chosen re-cipient of God's special favor and blessing. All others were foreigners to the covenants of the promise, without hope and without God in the world (Ephesians 2:12).

No country on earth – including, if not especially the United States – is a "godly nation." Nor can any geopolitical enti-ty claim divine preference over any other. With the end of the Jewish era came the end of all such national dealings in God's redemptive purposes.

The whole idea of a *"Christian nation"* is based on Dominion and Reconstruction theologies.[2]

AMERICA: NO MORE FAVORED BY GOD THAN ANY OTHER NATION

The Religious Right argues that, given its rich European and Christian heritage, America has been blessed by God be-cause of its adherence to Judeo-Christian values. They set America apart and above all other nations. This is heresy. We are no more favored by God than Russia, Cuba or Brazil. Such thinking is idolatrous.

Leaders of the Religious Right have waxed eloquent on their belief that America was founded as a "Christian" nation, but America never was, is not, and very likely never will be a Christian nation.

---

2. These are the *same* theologies that have influenced the *"Christianization"* of the American Revolution. They have at their root the Calvinist view of government, which teaches "The mission of the church is to renovate the world, including the state, according to Christian concepts. And the state is to assist the church in Christianizing the world. Consequently Calvin served as a political leader as well as a church leader in Geneva, and he saw no problem in using the machinery of the state to further his version of Christianity by punishing heretics, etc." John Eidsmor, *God & Caesar: Christian Faith & Political Action*, (Westchester, IL: Crossway, 1984) p. 14.

"Reclaiming America for Christ" presupposes that America was thoroughly Christian at one time, and that Christ wants it back. Both presuppositions are wrong.

Study the teachings of Jesus, and you will discover that He never intended His disciples to claim or reclaim nations for Himself.

The Christians in Uzbekistan do not expect their government to reflect their values. The believers in Egypt and elsewhere do not expect their government to reflect their values. The only people who expect their government to reflect their religious values are countries where religion and politics are synonymous. In Iran, the religious zealots expect the government to reflect Muslim values. But in America, where there is no systemic connection between religion and state, believers somehow expect the government to reflect their values. Are we looking for the Christian equivalent of a Muslim state? Do we want religious clerics dictating what we wear and what we do?

We should never expect our government to reflect our values. We should expect them to be hostile. This is what Jesus predicted.

Ed Dobson
Blinded by Might: Can the Religious Right Save America? (1999), pages 165-168

WHEN DID AMERICA BELONG TO GOD?

If we are to "take America *back* for God," it must have once "belonged" to God, but it's not at all clear when this golden Christian age was.

Were these God-glorifying years before, during or after Europeans "discovered" America and carried out the doctrine of "manifest destiny" – the belief that God had destined white Christians to conquer the native inhabitants and steal their land?

Were the God-glorifying years the ones in which whites massacred these natives by the millions, broke just about every covenant they ever made with them, and then forced survivors onto isolated reservations?

Were the God-glorifying years before, during or after white Christians loaded five to six million Africans on cargo ships to bring them to their newfound country, enslaving the three million or so who actually survived the brutal trip? Was it during the two centuries when Americans acquired remarkable wealth by the sweat and the blood of their slaves? Was this the time that we were truly "one nation under God," the blessed time that so many evangelicals seem to want to take our nation *back* to?

Gregory A. Boyd
The Myth of a Christian Nation, pages 98, 99

THE MAYFLOWER COMPACT

Concerning this query of a *"Christian nation,"* Albert James Dager helps to "clear the air," as it were. Concerning the famed "Mayflower Compact," he writes,

> Some of those aboard the Mayflower were Protestant Separatists which had fled England to Holland to escape persecution from the reformed Anglican Church prelates (an example of theonomy[3] at work), but the principals were men commissioned to further the business of the Virginia Company.

---

3. *i.e.,* Dominion and Reconstruction Theologies

The Mayflower Compact was an afterthought designed to keep the colony intact after they were blown off course from their intended landing at the mouth of the Hudson River, having landed instead at what later became Massachusetts. When they set sail, it was not a part of their original intent to draft the Mayflower Compact and form a Christian colony under its terms.

Although the document that the Mayflower passengers drew up did have some *influence* on the charters of a few colonies prior to the Revolutionary War, it had no *official* bearing on the federal government or on any of the colonies or states created either prior to or after the American Revolution. If we are going to call America a *Christian* nation we must see if its founding body, the Continental Congress, purposed to establish it as such. Did the body, in fact, "covenant" with God to form this nation?

When the Continental Congress drafted the Declaration of Independence and, later, the Congress formed under the Articles of Confederation drafted the Constitution of the United States of America, no mention was made of *Jesus Christ*. Rather, the only references to *deity* in the Declaration were to "God"[4]; none are in the Constitution. In fact, many of the framers of these documents were anti-Christian, being comprised of Masons, and deists of many persuasions.

It is apparent that the Western European influences that shaped America were part of what had become known as "*Christendom.*" But the history of Christendom is an ugly history fraught with tyranny and the enslavement of those who are "enlightened." If God gave the knowledge and means to subdue the earth and take dominion in the name of Jesus Christ, then that privilege has been terribly

---

4. The term "God," standing alone in a context, sits well with religions of the world. It does not prove anything to be "Christian."

abused. The fruit of Western Civilization, in spite of its enlightened accomplishments, demonstrates that no attempt to institute the Kingdom of God on earth before Jesus Christ returns can succeed. So the idea of a covenant between *any* nation and God is a fantasy.[5]

WHO REALLY PLACES PRESIDENTS AND KINGS IN POWER?

Those who have been influenced by the advocates of this *nationalized gospel* are often led to believe they will fail their God if they do not participate in campaign and voting processes and an "ungodly" candidate should happen to win.[6]

The implication, if not the actual teaching, is that it is always God's plan to have leaders with the right kind of "values" in power, and when His people fail to get them elected, His perfect will for that nation cannot be accomplished.

The plan of Him Who works out everything in conformity with the purpose of His will (Ephesians 1:11) is not so easily thwarted, and that includes the role world leaders play in the unfolding of His eternal purposes in Christ.

Whether a champion of good, or the very embodiment of evil (*e.g.* Hitler), no nation – including the United States – has ever had a president, dictator, king or emperor who was not placed in power by God's sovereign hand. And no such leader, good or evil, has ever been removed from power except as it has served God's eternal purpose.

It may have been hard to convince the oppressed Jews that it was God Who placed Pharaoh on his throne; yet, God proclaimed,

5. Albert James Dager, *Vengeance Is Ours* (Redmond, WA: Sword Publishers, 1990), pp. 220-221 (abridged).
6. See Appendix 3: *Jury Duty.*

I have raised you up for this very purpose, that I might display My power in you and that My name might be proclaimed in all the earth (Romans 9:17).

Nebuchadnezzar foolishly boasted,

Is not this the great Babylon I have built as the royal residence, by my might and power and for the glory of my majesty? (Daniel 4:30).

But the proud king was forced to eat grass like an animal to teach him that the Most High is sovereign over the kingdoms of men and gives them to anyone He wishes (Daniel 4:25). The lesson Nebuchadnezzar had to learn the hard way is one you and I should humbly accept:

> We should never expect our government to reflect our values. We should expect them to be hostile.
> — Ed Dobson

The Most High is sovereign over the kingdoms of men and gives them to anyone He wishes and sets over them the lowliest of men (Daniel 4:17).

While elections and other political mechanisms are the secondary causes involved in placing leaders in power, it is ultimately God Himself Who sets up kings and deposes them.

He changes the times and the seasons: He removes kings, and sets up kings (Daniel 2:21).

From a relative perspective, the nations of the earth are the enemies of Christ's kingdom and under the irrevocable curse of eventual destruction. No physical nation is excluded from that description, including the United States. All human efforts notwithstanding, fallen men cannot achieve peace within or between nations, nor raise themselves to a righteous standing before God, for God Himself has rendered failure certain.

THE SUCCESS OF THE GOSPEL

The success of Paul's Gospel has never been connected to the external moral virtues of any nation. On the contrary, his gospel has always been the most victorious in the face of severe persecution, and believers have been the strongest when faced, not with governmental approbation, but rather with oppression. We should never mislead people into thinking that the success and power of the gospel of grace depends on the moral rectitude of a nation. The power of this gospel lies in its true message, and in our boldness – in the face of any external circumstances – to proclaim that message to anyone who will listen.

Until Jesus returns, man's efforts will produce nothing but wars and rumors of wars, and we can expect that nation will rise against nation, and kingdom against kingdom (Matthew 24:6-7).

As Christ's ambassadors, we have not been commissioned to force moral bandages on a fatally wounded society, but simply to urge sinners to be reconciled to God (II Corinthians 5:20). Paul would not have had to look very hard to find a reason to stir up an outcry against the moral and governmental stench in Corinth, nor to encourage ousting its wicked politicians in favor of leaders with better "values," but he deliberately did neither. Instead, he went to that city resolved to know nothing except Jesus Christ and Him crucified (I Corinthians 2:2).

"Traditional Values"

To display the Ten Commandments on the wall of a public building or courthouse suggests that they have jurisdiction over the affairs conducted in that building. It also implies a commitment to comply with and prosecute its laws. In a syncretistic society composed of those who worship Allah, Buddha, Mammon and a thousand material idols, are we really prepared to enforce the command, *"You shall have no other gods before Me"*? Are we willing to prosecute and imprison those who misuse *"the name of the Lord your God"*?

The Ten Commandments were part of an exclusive covenant with Israel. Neither the promised blessing for keeping them nor the sure curses for breaking them were offered to or imposed on the rest of the nations, then or now.

The Ten Commandments also have no legal jurisdiction over the Body of Christ, for Christ cancelled the written code, with its regulations, that was against us and that stood opposed to us; He took it away, nailing it to the cross (Colossians 2:14).

The very fact that the Ten Commandments have become the common ground in this so-called "Judeo-Christian heritage" betrays a tragic paradox. As believers, we need to face the sad fact that there simply is no room for the gospel in such an alleged common heritage. To the degree that "Judeo" is emphasized, "Christian" must be suppressed. Likewise, to the degree that "Christian" is stressed, the "Judeo" part must be suppressed. The only way that "Judeo" and "Christian" elements can unite, therefore, is by adopting a common religious-political moral code – minus Jesus Christ. How can any true believer think that God is pleased by efforts to mold the United States into a society espousing a "Judeo-Christian heritage" when, to accomplish that misguided objective, His Son must be left out in order to hold its conflicting components together? "God & Country"? or Christ's Kingdom?

> *Who has delivered us from the power of darkness, and has translated us into the kingdom of His dear Son* (Colossians 1:13).

> *That you would walk worthy of God, Who has called you unto His kingdom and glory* (I Thessalonians 2:12).

Paul does not address believers in terms of national identity, but as being *"translated … into the kingdom of His dear Son."* Those who have been baptized by one Spirit into His one Body (I Corinthians 12:13) are neither Jew nor Greek (Galatians 3:28). We have become the Body of the exalted and risen Head, Jesus Christ.

On our behalf, God has placed all things under the feet of His Son and appointed Him to be Head over everything for us, the church, which is His Body (Ephesians 1:22-23).

Christ's *present* reign does not have as its primary concern earthly nations, but rather the kingdom given to Him by His Father. Nor do His people have as their primary concern the affairs of this world, but rather the interests of the kingdom of their Lord and Savior. Their business is not to promote human national agendas, but the objectives of *"the kingdom of His dear Son"* into which we have been translated.

Whatever days God may require believers to spend as aliens and sojourners in this sin-cursed world should be spent as a living sacrifice, wholly committed to carrying out the implications of *"the kingdom of His dear Son."*

The agenda to "turn our nation back to its Judeo-Christian heritage" espoused by so many church leaders, therefore, is not a mandate from Christ, and can only serve to deflect His people from the responsibilities He has revealed and entrusted to them.

POLITICAL REFORMS

Many dear saints of the past and present feel called upon to give their lives to the physical welfare of their fellows, especially by introducing reforms in government, and even opposing rule which they think harmful. But once we see God's great object in human government, that it is to *humble* humanity, and so to lead them to rely alone on Him, then we see the reason *why* we are exhorted to be subject to the superior authorities, and understand *how* it is that there is *no* authority except under God (Romans 13:2).

In the United States voices are loud in urging Christians to combine in order to control the government and save it from corruption and godlessness. They point to the failure of the church in Europe to take an active part in opposing oppression and preventing war, and call upon the religious people to use their influence in creating a new world. Little do they realize that this will develop into the worst of all world powers that have ever afflicted mankind! Terrestrial rule is not for us. Our realm is in the heavens.

A.E. Knoch (1874-1965)
Unsearchable Riches, Volume 38, pages 220, 221, 230

TO WHICH POLITICAL PARTY
DOES GOD BELONG?

As we have contemplated these issues, we have become increasingly convinced that it is a serious mistake for believers to identify with any political party or "ism" in this world. Rather than showing a commitment to certain causes, or identification with a particular political party, this has the effect of compromising the effectiveness of Christ's gospel.

Political affiliations are a source of much strife and conten-
tion all over the world. Should we not, therefore, avoid unnecessary alienation by not wearing such political convictions on our sleeves?

By aligning ourselves with a particular political party, we often unwittingly alienate those who may identify with an opposing party, thus unnecessarily erecting a stumbling block
that can only hinder the credibility of the gospel of our Lord
Jesus Christ.

To the Jews Paul became like a Jew to win the Jews. To the weak
he became as weak to win the weak. He became all things to
all men that he might save some. This he did for the sake of the
gospel committed to his trust (I Corinthians 9:20-23).

Even among believers, do you think political polarization
would aid, or hinder, our willingness to make every effort to
keep the unity of the Spirit through the bond of peace (Ephesians 4:3)?

OUR CONFIDENCE

Many Christians have been duped into thinking that some
sort of national renewal will come if we simply get more
people registered to vote, elect the right candidates in office
and pass legislation in line with the "Judeo-Christian heritage." Christian political activism is viewed as critical for the
future of our country. For the Christian to place any hope
in political systems is naïve at best, and will only bring disappointment and disillusionment. Our confidence must not
rest in such human devices, but in the power of the gospel to
transform hearts in any culture.

*We ... worship God in the spirit, and rejoice in Christ Je-
sus, and have no confidence in the flesh* (Philippians 3:3).

Fear the LORD and the king; and meddle not with them who are given to change (Proverbs 24:21).

Since Constantine, the Church has taken part in earth's politics, with very evil results, and now Protestantism, like Catholicism, threatens to take a large hand in controlling the "temporal powers," in order to make a new world.

A.E. Knoch (1874-1965)
Unsearchable Riches
Volume 38, pages 8, 9

Chapter 11

Patriotism and Meddling in Politics

POLITICAL ACTIVISM[1]

*T*he very premise that believers have some kind of spiritual duty to actively participate in human campaign and voting processes begs closer scrutiny.[2] Are we somehow obligated to join forces with those who are trying to oust the bad guys and replace them with leaders who supposedly share our "values"? The popular notion that political activism is God's appointed means for bringing "moral" reform to our country certainly has its zealous advocates, but their zeal is not based on knowledge (Romans 10:2).

For the most part, such teaching is gleaned from Old Testament passages that have not been properly filtered through the lens of Paul's Gospel. When the Old Testament is not understood under the greater light of the revelation given to

---

1. This section, "Political Activism," is taken from *Bible Students Notebook #223*, adapted from the writings of Jon Zens and Cliff Bjork, *God and Country: The Dangers of Contemporary Christian Americanism*.
2. See Appendix 3: *Jury Duty*

Paul, it can be a veritable mine of "proof texts" providing apparent justification for all kinds of sociological, political, or even military actions aimed at combating evil.

> We who live in America today are so addicted to our idols of freedom and materialism.
>
> — John Saunders

Why stop at merely deposing "ungodly" leaders? Using the Old Testament as our national "moral" guide, let's advocate stoning to death our unruly children, adulterers, Sabbath breakers, worshippers of false Gods, those who seek the counsel of demonic spirits, and even those who blaspheme by taking the Lord's name in vain. These are also "moral" laws included in the Old Testament canon and their execution would certainly have an impact on our society.

The end of the preceding paragraph may sound facetious, but it is not such a large step from involvement in political activism to participation in these more extreme measures. It is a line that is crossed by those who fire-bomb abortion clinics, or who attack other societal evils with similar tactics, often in God's name. Paul provides no warrant for the kinds of political activism and disruptive protests in which believers are often encouraged to participate.

Rather than to rail against the alleged abuses of our leaders, he teaches us to pray humbly for kings and all those in authority, that we may live peaceful and quiet lives (I Timothy 2:2).

NATIONAL PRIDE AND PATRIOTISM

Loyalty and allegiance are gripping words, are they not? They represent a concept that most of us were introduced to at an early age. Prior to his conversion Paul was a man who had great pride in his nation (Philippians 3:5).

If ever there was a nation to be proud of would it not have been the one that God established, God's nation? Yet upon meeting the Lord Jesus Christ, Paul's attention was captivated and his pride and allegiance changed!

> *I count all things but loss for the excellency of the knowledge of Christ Jesus my Lord: for Whom I have suffered the loss of all things, and do count them but dung, that I may win Christ* (Philippians 3:8).

> *God forbid that I should glory, except in the cross of our Lord Jesus Christ, by Whom the world is crucified unto me, and I unto the world* (Galatians 6:14).

WRAPPED IN THE RED, WHITE AND BLUE

A politicized faith not only blurs our priorities, but weakens our loyalties. The language of our spiritual citizenship frequently gets wrapped in the red, white and blue. Rather than acting as resident aliens of

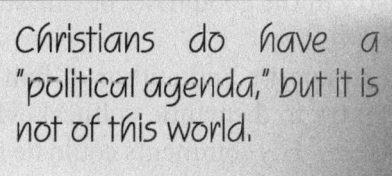

Christians do have a "political agenda," but it is not of this world.

— David C. Pack

a heavenly kingdom, too often we sound like resident apologists for a Christian America. Unless we reject the false reliance on the illusion of Christian America, we will continue to distort the gospel and thwart a genuine biblical identity.

John Seel (1953)
The Evangelical Pulpit (1993), pages 106-107

SALVATION BY POLITICAL ELECTION?

The far right of the evangelical movement in the United States has a highly organized campaign to impose biblical law on every aspect of American society. There is a growing emphasis on preaching that it is time to save America – not soul by soul, but election by election. All the while, with on-going organized protests, fiery pulpit preaching and political debates, Christians are being seen as aggressive, intolerant, hateful, hypocritical, self-righteous trouble makers.

> A politicized faith not only blurs our priorities, but weakens our loyalties.
>
> — John Seel

It is quite interesting to me that Jesus had very little to say about the political power of His day, Rome. The writers of the New Testament launched no bold attack on Rome's politics. "Legislating morality" was not a platform for Jesus or the apostles in their ministry in the good news of Christ.

Paul, an apostle and author of half of the New Testament, did not try to dismantle cultural evils, a prime example being slavery. His comments could be interpreted as though he endorsed the idea of a man owning his brother. However, he only encouraged slaves to be Christians, peaceful, and to be good to their masters. This type of behavior is in the spirit of what Jesus taught when He said, *"Love your enemies."*

Paul Vieira
Jesus Has Left the Building, pages 264-265

A Political Savior

The era of the Gentiles has a purpose which is the opposite of that of the Kingdom of God. Then, God will display what He can do, through His Own Anointed. Now, however, it is necessary to expose the futility and the incapacity and the failure of human government apart from the direct supervision of the Deity. Even men with the noblest motives, with extraordinary capacity and possessing brilliant minds, are hampered and frustrated in their attempts to give the people the plenty and the peace for which these men strive, for their efforts are out of season.

Great as are the hardships and the calamities which come to earth's inhabitants because of the shortcomings of man's rule over man, it would be an infinitely greater calamity if men could succeed in ruling perfectly apart from God. That would make them independent, self-centered, self-sufficient, so that God would become nothing to them, rather than their All. Just as it is necessary for a sinner to realize his need of a personal Savior, so it is essential that the nations learn their need of a political Savior.

> The more political one becomes, the more one hates.

A.E. Knoch (1874-1965)
Concordant Studies in the Book of Daniel

Political Christianity

Jesus answered, "My kingdom is not of this world. If My kingdom were of this world, My deputies, also, would have contended, lest I should be given up to the Jews. Yet now is My kingdom not hence" (John 18:36).

The Lord's kingdom was not of this world then, and neither is it now. When Peter picked up the sword in Gethsemane, Jesus rebuked him. Jesus would have rebuked any man then who would have fought to rescue Him. Such fighters would have sadly mistaken this present world system as the field of His reign. In spite of overwhelming scriptural testimony, many today still think that His kingdom is of this world. Instead of trying to rescue Him from the Jews, they are trying to rescue Him from errant political forces. They are striving to make sure that He has a clean world system in which to establish His government. But He is not going to use this world system to establish His government. Again, His government is not of this world.

> You can safely assume that you've created God in your own image when it turns out that God hates all the same people you do.
>
> — Anne Lamott

Political Christianity is doubly ignorant. Not only is it like the housewife who hurries to clean the house before the maid comes (why does she think the maid is coming?), but it is cleaning the wrong house.

Martin Zender
Clanging Gong News (Volume 1, No. 10)
"Cleaning the Wrong House"

Political Activism

We can't protect or expand the cause of Christ by human political and social activism, no matter how great or sincere the efforts. Ours is a spiritual battle waged against worldly ideologies and dogmas arrayed against God, and we achieve victory over them only with the weapon of Scripture. The apostle Paul writes:

> *Though we walk in the flesh, we do not war after the flesh: (For the weapons of our warfare are not carnal, but mighty through God to the pulling down of strong holds;) Casting down imaginations, and every high thing that exalts itself against the knowledge of God, and bringing into captivity every thought to the obedience of Christ* (II Corinthians 10:3-5).

God is not calling us to wage a culture war that would seek to transform our countries into "Christian nations." To devote all, or even most, of our time, energy, money and strategy to putting a facade of morality on the world or over our governmental and political institutions is to badly misunderstand our roles as Christians in a spiritually lost world.

A stance that emphasizes political activism and social moralizing always diverts energy and resources ... Such an antagonistic position toward the

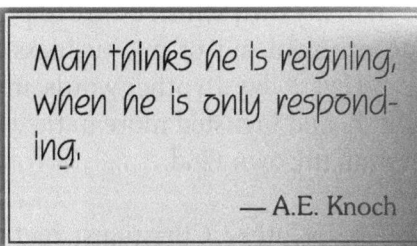

Man thinks he is reigning, when he is only responding.

— A.E. Knoch

established secular culture invariably leads believers to feel hostile not only to unsaved government leaders with whom they disagree, but also antagonistic toward the unsaved residents of that culture – neighbors and fellow citizens they ought to love, pray for, and share the gospel with. To me it is unthinkable that we become enemies of the very people we seek to win to Christ.

John MacArthur
Pulpit Magazine (October 2008)

GOD IS NOT A REPUBLICAN

In the fall of 2000, I was a campaign worker for the George W. Bush campaign. At that particular time in my life, my heart was far from the Lord and I needed something to fill the void. I can remember making phone calls and telling people that Governor Bush was the answer to America's problems. I told them that Bush would restore integrity back

> If any President or other governmental authority is elected or removed from office, it's God's will that has been carried out.

to the White House and would work hard to lower our taxes and restore confidence back to our military. Four years later, I realized that my so-called "noble" desire for lower taxes, less government, and a more powerful military was nothing more than my own selfish desire to pad my own pocket, keep the government out of my business, and help me feel safe each and every day. In other words, my goal was to satisfy my own flesh, and I trusted more in the provision of the government than my own God.

I, like many other Christians, had fallen for the lie that Christianity and Republicanism (or Conservatism if you like) were compatible – and even ideologically equal. However, nothing could be further from the truth. We have been deceived into thinking that God is going to somehow use the Republican Party to bring in His Kingdom. Is it really God's policy for the Christian to support the lowering of taxes so "Americans can keep their own money?" Does God really want Christians to pursue the idea that we should have lesser government in order to "give more power to the people?" Is it God's purpose for the Church to be in support of a stronger military and promote the spending of billions of dollars on weapons programs when there are people all over the world who are homeless and starving? Are these the things we should be concerning ourselves with? Are these Christian principles? Well, they certainly are the principles of the Republican Party, but I see nowhere in Scripture where God wants us to pursue these things. God wants us to pursue those things that are *"lovely, pure, and of good report"* (Philippians 4:8). He wants us to be consumed with living the gospel of Christ, not the external reformation of a culture.

I must add that God is not a Democrat either. He is neither a Libertarian, a Constitutionalist, nor a member of the Green Party.

Ken Eckerty
God is Not a Republican

GOD IS NOT AN AMERICAN

Not only is God not a member of a political party, He is also not an American. *"God is no respecter of persons,"* and yet while we are bombing and killing Iraqi citizens, Christians

> Men never do evil so completely and cheerfully as when they do it from a religious conviction.
>
> — Blaise Pascal

have no problem promoting the slogan "God bless America" while hanging American flags from their houses and cars, and at the same time telling others that we must "pray for our troops." What about God blessing Iraq? Has God forgotten them? What about praying for the poor in this world? Is God concerned that Iraqi men (women and children) are dying, or is it only "our troops" that concern Him?

God loves Americans, but He also loves Iraqis, Palestinians, Russians and Chinese. I am aware that most Christians understand this; however, I'm not sure we are living this principle. We must stop this promotion of America. It is not America, but Jesus Christ we should be promoting. He is the source of our life and the focus of our vision!

Ken Eckerty
God is not a Republican

AN IDOLATROUS CELEBRATION

Shortly after the Gulf War in 1992 I happened to visit a July Fourth worship service at a certain megachurch. At center stage in this auditorium stood a large cross next to an equally large American flag. The congregation sang praise choruses mixed with such patriotic hymns as "God Bless America." The climax of the service centered on a video of a well-known Christian military general giving a patriotic speech about how God has blessed America and blessed its military troops, as evidenced by the speedy and almost "casualty-free" victory "He gave us" in the Gulf War (Iraqi deaths apparently weren't counted as "casualties" worthy of notice). Triumphant military music played in the background as he spoke.

> Things today are exactly where God intends them to be.
>
> — A.E. Knoch

The video closed with a scene of a silhouette of three crosses on a hill with an American flag waving in the background. Majestic, patriotic music now thundered. Suddenly, four fighter jets appeared on the horizon, flew over the crosses, and then split apart. As they roared over the camera, the words "God Bless America" appeared on the screen it front of the crosses.

The congregation responded with roaring applause, catcalls, and a standing ovation. I saw several people wiping tears from their eyes. Indeed, as I remained frozen in my seat, I grew teary-eyed as well – but for entirely different reasons. I was struck with horrified grief.

Thoughts raced through my mind: How could the cross and the sword have been so thoroughly fused without anyone seeming to notice?

> The "best" man for the job will never be elected. This would run contrary to God's present purpose.

How could Jesus' self-sacrificial death be linked with flying killing machines? How could Calvary be associated with bombs and missiles? How could Jesus' people applaud tragic violence, regardless of why it happened and regardless of how they might benefit from its outcome? How could the kingdom of God be reduced to this sort of violent, nationalistic tribalism? Has the church progressed at all since the Crusades?

Indeed, I wondered how this tribalistic, militaristic, religious celebration was any different from the one I had recently witnessed on television carried out by the Taliban Muslims raising their guns as they joyfully praised Allah for the victories they believed "he had given them" in Afghanistan?

This is the way *all* versions of the kingdom of the world operate.

Gregory A. Boyd
The Myth of a Christian Nation, pages 87-89

"Good Causes" Are a Distraction

There are many "good causes" being championed in the world today that frequently serve as distractions for the Christian, because they draw our attention away from our true calling. In most cases there is no question that the issues are just and right, but they only deal with the symptoms – they leave the disease untouched. For centuries the church has been offering the world band-aids for a deep, mortal wound.

Rick Joyner
There Were Two Trees in the Garden (1986)

> I am not a politician. I have never voted. But I am going to be a politician in the future.
>
> — A.E. Knoch

Not a Calling, but a Diverson

Even the noblest political causes can be a form of corruption when they divert our attention and effort from the work of Jesus in the world. For believers, this vision of worldly power is not a calling, but a distraction – another case of the good being the enemy of the best. It is a temptation Jesus rejected – not because it was dangerous, but because it was trivial compared with His greater mission.

Cal Thomas
Blinded by Might: Can the Religious Right Save America? (1999), page 94

The Constantine Mindset

Constantine legalized Christianity in A.D. 313, and because of its association with him, the religion immediately exploded in popularity. Within seventy years it was proclaimed the official religion of the Roman Empire – making it a crime *not* to be a Christian. The first recorded instance of Christians killing pagans occurred shortly after. In short order, the militant church extended its power by conquering lands and peoples throughout Europe, compelling them to become baptized Christians or die. As Charlemagne instructed his Christian troops in their conquest of the Saxons: "If there is anyone of the Saxon people lurking among them unbaptized, and if he scorns to come to baptism … and stay a pagan, let him die."

The church had become "the church militant and triumphant."

What followed was a long and terrible history of people using the sword "in Jesus' name for the glory of God." Though there are, of course, many wonderful examples of Christ-like people and movements throughout church history, the reigning church as a whole – "Christendom" – acted about as badly as most versions of the kingdoms of the world.

> Man's way may seem to be leading to a hopeless end; but God's way actually leads to an endless hope.

Augustine was the first theologian to align the church in an official way with the use of the sword, and it happened to be against a fellow Christian group, the Donatists. Among other things, the Donatists believed that the alliance between the church and the state that had been forged since Constantine was undermining the purity and integrity of the church, and they wanted to keep the church pure.

Augustine now justified the use of force by arguing that inflicting temporal pain to help someone avoid eternal pain is justified. Since God had given the church the power of the sword, Augustine reasoned, it had a responsibility to use it to further God's purposes in the world just as a stern father has a responsibility to beat his child for his own good. Since God sometimes uses terror for the good of humans, we who are God's representatives on earth – the church – may use terror for the sake of the gospel. If the end justifies it, the use of violence as a means to that end is justified. (This is, in essence, Augustine's "just war" policy.) Augustine thus invoked a recent edict of the emperor Theodosius to criminalize the "heresy" of Donatism and attempt to persecute it out of existence. This set a tragic precedent for handling doctrinal disagreements for the next thirteen hundred years.

Throughout the Middle Ages and into the Renaissance, millions were burned at the stake, hung, beheaded or executed in other ways for resisting some aspect of the church's teaching or for failing to operate under its authority. Thousands upon thousands were tortured in unthinkable ways in an attempt to elicit a confession of faith in the Savior and the church; some of the macabre torturing devices were even inscribed with the logo "Glory be only to God." Christian groups such as the Paulicians, Cathars, Albigensians and Waldensians were massacred by the towns – often including women and children – and Christians in both the West and the East slaughtered each other in Jesus' name as ruthlessly as they slaughtered Muslims. Terrible atrocities were carried out on Jews, especially when the Crusades needed to be financed, and multitudes of women (estimates range between sixty thousand to several million) were burned or hung for allegedly being witches – most of whom denied the charge. The church of resident aliens had become a horde of savage warlords.

The militant, Constantine mindset carried into the Protestant Reformation. So long as they remained a persecuted minority, Reformers generally decried the use of violence for religious purposes. But once given the power of the sword, most used it as relentlessly as it had previously been used against them. Indeed, with the exception of the Anabaptist, every splinter group of the Reformation in the sixteenth and seventeenth centuries spilled blood. Lutherans, Calvinists, Anglicans and other Protestant groups fought each other, fought the Catholics, and martyred Anabaptists and other "heretics" by the hundreds. It wasn't until the bloodshed became economically unbearable and unfeasible in the Thirty Years' War that a truce (the Peace of Westphalia) was called and Christians agreed, at least theoretically, to end the violence.

Yet while the Christian use of the sword subsided in Europe, it continued in the New World. As God gave Canaan to Joshua, many argued, so God gave other lands over to white European Christians. To the thinking of many, the church "militant and triumphant" was on the move to conquer the world for Christ, and all who resisted it were seen as resisting God Himself and deserving of death. Christians coming to the long-inhabited land of America participated in the slaughter of millions of Native Americans, as well as the enslavement and murder of millions of Africans as a means of conquering and establishing this new land for Jesus. Such, it was claimed, was the "manifest destiny" of Europeans, and it wasn't simply warriors who died at the swords of Christians. As is common with kingdom-of-the-world conquests, raping, torturing for sport, pillaging and treatise breaking were widespread.

While the violent expression of the Constantine mindset has been largely outlawed, the mindset itself is very much alive today. To be sure, in some parts of the world Christians still engage in violence against other Christians, Muslims, Hindus and other groups. But even within the borders of America, the mindset is alive and well. When Jerry Falwell, reflecting a widespread sentiment among conservative Christians, says America should hunt terrorists down and "blow them all away in the name of the Lord," he is expressing the Constantine mindset. When Pat Robertson declared that the United States should assassinate President Chavez of Venezuela, he also is expressing the Constantine mindset. And when Christians try to enforce their holy will on select groups of sinners by power of law, they are essentially doing the same thing, even if the violent means of enforcing their will is no longer available to them.

Gregory A. Boyd
The Myth of a Christian Nation (2005), pages 76-80

THE TIT-FOR-TAT KINGDOM

It's hard not to get pulled into the passions that fuel the violence of the kingdom of the world. Indeed, the demonic, tribalistic passion that sets "us" over against "them" *seems* completely natural to us. If you hit me, my natural instinct is to hit you back – not turn the other cheek! Tit-for-tat, eye-for-an-eye, tooth-for-a-tooth – this is what makes the bloody kingdom of the world go around.

Gregory A. Boyd
The Myth of a Christian Nation (2005), page 24

TAKING BACK AMERICA FOR GOD

We have become intoxicated with the Constantinian, nationalistic, violent mindset of imperialistic Christendom ... The evidence of this is all around but nowhere clearer than in the simple, oft-repeated slogan that we Christians are going to "take America back for God." The thinking is that America was founded as a Christian nation but has simply veered off track. If we can just get the power of Caesar again, however, we can take it back. If we can just get more Christians into office, pass more Christian laws, support more Christian policies, we can restore this nation to its "one nation under

God" status … If we look at historic reality rather than pious verbiage, it's obvious that America never really "belonged to God."… There was nothing distinctively Christ-like about the way America was "discovered," conquered, or governed in the early years. To the contrary, the way this nation was "discovered," conquered, and governed was a rather typical, barbaric, violent, kingdom-of-the-world affair … The fact that it was largely done under the banner of Christ doesn't make it more Christian, any more than any other bloody conquest done in Jesus' name throughout history (such as the Crusades and the Inquisition) qualifies them as Christ-like.

Gregory A. Boyd
The Myth of a Christian Nation (2005), pages 90-91, 99

THE SERIOUS DANGER OF GOVERNMENT IN THE NAME OF GOD

"Theocracy" is the worst of all governments. If we must have a tyrant, a robber baron is far better than an inquisitor. The baron's cruelty may sometimes sleep … but the inquisitor who mistakes his own cruelty and lust of power and fear for the voice of Heaven will torment us infinitely, because he torments us with the approval of his own conscience and his better impulses appear to him as temptations. And since Theocracy is the worst, the nearer any government approaches to Theocracy the worse it will be.

Of all tyrannies a tyranny sincerely exercised for the good of its victims may be the most oppressive. It may be better to live under robber barons than under omnipotent moral busybodies.

C.S. Lewis (1898-1963)
Of Other Worlds (page 81)
The Humanitarian Theory of Punishment (June 1953)

OUR REALM OF VICTORY

Our realm of victory is not to be found in an earthly focus,

> *We look not at the things which are seen, but at the things which are not seen: for the things which are seen are temporary; but the things which are not seen last for the ages* (II Corinthians 4:18).

Or in a carnal battle,

> *We wrestle not against flesh and blood, but against principalities, against powers, against the rulers of the darkness of this world, against spiritual wickedness in heavenly places* (Ephesians 6:12).

Or by a fleshly means,

> *We are the circumcision, who worship God in the spirit, and rejoice in Christ Jesus, and have no confidence in the flesh* (Philippians 3:3).

No, our realm of victory is in the spiritual domain, and it is found totally in the *Person* of our Lord Jesus Christ! He *is* our victory and triumph!

> *Now thanks be to God, Who always causes us to triumph in Christ, and makes manifest the savor of His knowledge by us in every place* (II Corinthians 2:14).

> *Thanks be to God, Who gives us the victory through our Lord Jesus Christ* (I Corinthians 15:57).

Since all of this is true, then we cannot lower ourselves to the earthly, physical, carnal, fleshly means of the political-warfare system of this evil age's course. Indeed, we have been marvelously delivered from such a plight, and called to a far higher realm!

Well has Theodore Austin-Sparks (1888-1971) written,

> Insofar as we become involved in the matters of the kingdoms of this world, we lose our magnetic vocation, and we shall involve ourselves in chaos from which it will take a very great deal to extricate us.[3]

> That has been the historic tragedy of Christendom: it has in various ways become linked up with the kingdoms and interests of this world, and that is the secret of its spiritual ineffectiveness. The Church, which is Christ's Body, is a heavenly thing since Christ, its Head, has ascended, and all that comes down into and through His Body is heavenly in source and nature. This is utterly different from the things of earth.

> Moreover, the Church is not here to establish or extend the Kingdom of Heaven in the earth. It is here to testify of the Lord Jesus Christ, to establish a testimony in the nations, and to gather to itself members. The Kingdom of Heaven is for a later time.[4]

THE REVOLUTION OF JESUS CHRIST

Though sympathizing with the revolutionaries' analysis of what was wrong with society, and in fact being mistaken for

---

3. Some believers, even some "Christian ministers" lose sight of their *heavenly purpose* and focus on earthly things. One "church," for example, publishes a monthly periodical that passes through my mail box. It is not sent out by a political organization, but is clearly marked: "published monthly by _____ _____ Church." The latest issue that I have on my desk will serve as an example of its *focus*. There are thirty-four (34) articles in this *church* publication, twenty-five of them are *political/governmental* in nature. That means that seventy-five percent (75%) of its contents are *devoted* to these issues.

4. T. Austin-Sparks, *A Witness and a Testimony*, July 1927.

a revolutionary Himself by the political authorities of His day, nevertheless Jesus did not advocate a new political regime to be established by force through revolutionary action. He called for the love of our enemies, not their destruction; for readiness to suffer, instead of using force; for forgiveness, instead of hate and revenge. One might even say Jesus was more revolutionary than the revolutionaries, or revolutionary in a very different way. The revolution He had in mind was a radical change of heart on the part of mankind, involving conversion away from selfishness and toward the willing service of God and of people in general.

Clark H. Pinnock
Reason Enough (1980)

Christians who condone the warfare state and its nebulous crusades against "evil" have been duped. There is nothing "Christian" about the state's aggressive militarism, its senseless wars, its interventions into the affairs of other countries, and its expanding empire.

Laurence M. Vance
Christianity and War
2005, page ix

Chapter 12

The Warfare State

Warfare a False System

*J*s not the whole system of war in this age of grace just one more false system? It is a system set up against flesh and blood, using for its weapons carnal things. In essence it is the ultimate *un*grace act. Warfare is contrary to everything that God is instructing us to be. It calls us to perform the most unchristian acts conceivable. War causes those of a baser nature to sink even lower as the recent prison abuse scandals in both the U.K. and the U.S.A. attest.

Bill Petri
War and Grace (2006)

Ridding the World of Evil

Fallen humans tend to identify their own group as righteous and any group that opposes them as evil. If *they* were not evil, we tend to believe, no conflict would exist. Hence, the only way to end the conflict is to "rid the world of this evil," as President George W. Bush said after the terrorist attack on the World Trade Center. The "good" (our tribe) must extinguish the "evil" (their tribe), using all means necessary, including violence. This is the age-old myth of *redemptive violence*.

Gregory A. Boyd
The Myth of a Christian Nation (2005), page 26

RELIGIOUS WARMONGERS

In 2003, on the eve of the second US attack on Iraq, Rev. John Hagee held hands with Rev. Benny Hinn, praying for war, in the name of Jesus:

> I pray for our President ... that you would give him the wisdom of Solomon to lead this nation into war against the enemies of righteousness ... I pray God that the enemy shall be destroyed and that the angels of heaven go before the U.S. and British forces bringing deliverance to that part of the world and, most assuredly, deliverance to Israel. ... in Jesus name. Amen.[1]

PEACE THROUGH VIOLENCE?

Any peace achieved by violence is a peace forever threatened by violence, thus ensuring that the bloody game will be perpetuated. Followers of Jesus must realize – and must help others realize – that the hope of the world lies not in any particular version of the kingdom of the world gaining the upper hand in Babylon's endless tit-for-tat game. The hope of the world lies in a kingdom that is not of this world, a kingdom that doesn't participate in tit-for-tat, a kingdom that operates with a completely different understanding of power.

Gregory A. Boyd
The Myth of a Christian Nation (2005), page 27

---

1. Tom Compton, *Praying for War, In the Name of Jesus.*

How to Get a War to Work

To get a war to work – to get men to kill other men that have never aggressed against them and that they don't even know – the state must do two things: (1) convince men to love the state and (2) to hate the members of other states. The first is always cloaked in *patriotism,* and leads to an acceptance of *interventionism.* The second is always cloaked in *nationalism,* and leads to *hatred* toward foreigners within one's country.

Laurence M. Vance
Christianity and War (2005), page 88

Christians in the Military

Let all bitterness, and wrath, and anger, and clamor, and evil speaking, be put away from you, with all malice: and be ye kind one to another, tenderhearted, forgiving one another, even as God for Christ's sake hath forgiven you. Be ye therefore followers of God, as dear children; And walk in love, as Christ also hath loved us, and hath given Himself for us an offering and a sacrifice to God for a sweet-smelling savor (Ephesians 4:31-5:2).

> Don't waste time fighting the darkness. Just bask in the light. Light swallows up darkness.

There is an alternative to this ceaseless, bloody merry-go-round: it is the kingdom of God. It is to live the life of Jesus Christ to opt out of the kingdom-of-the-world war machine and manifest a radically different, beautiful, loving way of life. To refuse to kill for patriotic reasons is to show "we actually take our identity in Christ more seriously than our identity with the empire, the nation-state, or the ethnic terror cell whence we come," as Lee Camp says.[2]

So, while I respect the sincerity and courage of Christians who may disagree and feel it their duty to defend their country with violence, I honestly see no way to condone a Christian's decision to kill on behalf of any country – or for any other reason.

> It would be an infinitely greater calamity if men could succeed in ruling perfectly apart from God.
>
> — A.E. Knoch

Gregory A. Boyd
The Myth of a Christian Nation (2005), page 173

CHRISTIAN KILLERS

There is no doubt that many of the soldiers responsible for the recent death and destruction in Fallujah are Christians. And there is no doubt that many Americans who call for more death and destruction in Iraq and elsewhere are Christians as well.

Christian Killers.

The phrase should be a contradiction in terms. If someone referred to Christian adulterers ... most Christians would get an extremely perplexed look on their face. But when Christians in the military continue killing for the state, and Christians not in the military call for more killing in the name of the state, many Christians don't even raise an eyebrow.

Laurence M. Vance
Christianity and War (2005), page 24

---

2. Lee Camp, *Mere Discipleship*, page 148

WAR AND THE CHRISTIANS

The early Christians were wholly opposed to warfare and violence. They were certainly not cowards, while they refused to serve in the Roman army they apparently did not flinch from lions in the arena, or being beheaded, rather than kill a fellow human being.

Bill Petri
War and Grace (2006)

WAR AGAINST TERRORISM

Christians who support or remain silent about Bush's "war against terrorism" are terribly inconsistent. If the state were to say, "Here Christian, put on this uniform, take this gun, go to your hometown, and kill your father," Christians would recoil in horror and refuse to obey the state. But if the state were to say, "Here Christian, put on this uniform, take this gun, go to Iraq, and kill someone else's father," I am afraid that many Christians would reply, "When does my plane leave?"

Why is it that the same Christian, who would not do the former, has no qualms about doing the latter?

Laurence M. Vance
Christianity and War (2005), page 27

WAR PERPETUATES HATRED

The recent war on terror that the United States finds itself engaged in has not decreased terrorist activity, but rather has seen it escalate to the highest levels ever known. Bloodshed creates more bloodshed, which creates more hatred, which ensures more violence, and hatred. This is what waging a physical war produces. Its end is never good, and it never brings peace that can last. The United States is not eliminating terrorists, but with every act of violence they create more terrorists, who hate Americans more than the ones who preceded them. The whole world system is fortified against Christ; and the peoples of the earth have been engaged in little else than in raising and strengthening such strongholds for the space of 6,000 years. The doctrine of grace goes forth against all the combined and concentrated powers of resistance of the whole world; and the warfare is to be waged against every strongly fortified place of error and of sin in the spiritual realm. These strong fortifications of error and of sin are to be battered down and laid in ruins by our spiritual weapons of knowledge, longsuffering, kindness, love and the Holy Spirit as we have already seen.

Bill Petri
War and Grace (2006)

Understanding Muslim Contempt

Historically, the most prominent of church-ordained "just wars" were the crusades of 1095-1291 C.E. The Roman Catholic Church has not given any apology or expression of remorse for the crusades; they are still considered to be just wars. Using "crusade" terminology today shows an utter disregard for the atrocities committed during the crusades and a lack of understanding at the Muslim contempt for "Christian" nations, which became ingrained because of those atrocities. Many historians even take the position that the Crusades actually helped Islam become a viable religion in the Middle East, by uniting Muslims against a common enemy.

Heads of state with heavy Christian populations have used the rhetoric of just war since the term was first used in order to gain favor for military operations. Once a war is declared "just," all moral obligation seemingly disappears and Christians can support and even become combatants for the cause.

The Middle East harbors grudges against Christians and Jews, which date back to the Crusades. Our wars have created a gap, which only the grace of God can bridge. While we may be able to free some Muslims from tyrannical regimes, this good does not counteract the evils and hatred we spawn from our military activities there.

Bill Petri
War and Grace (2006)

ISLAMIC ANIMOSITY

Much of the profound animosity Islamic terrorists feel towards "satanic" America is fueled by a cultural memory of what Christians did to Muslims during the Crusades. Believing that America is a Christian nation, they di-

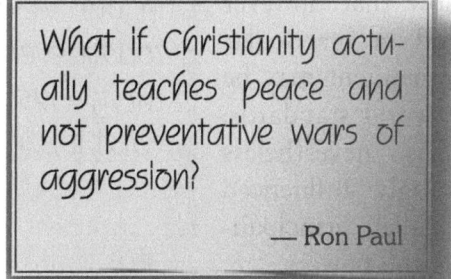

What if Christianity actually teaches peace and not preventative wars of aggression?

— Ron Paul

rect their collective, historically acquired hatred toward it.

The Christian version of the kingdom of the world was actually the *worst* version the world has ever seen. For this was the version of the kingdom of the world that did the most harm to the kingdom of God. Not only did it torture and kill, as versions of the kingdom of the world frequently do – it did this under the banner of Christ. If violence and oppression are demonic, violence and oppression "in the name of Jesus" is far more so. The church of Christendom thereby brought disrepute to the name of Christ, associating His kingdom with the atrocities it carried out for centuries. The resistance most Islamic countries have to Christianity today, in fact, is partly to be explained by the vicious behavior of Christians toward Muslims throughout history.

Gregory A. Boyd
The Myth of a Christian Nation (2005), pages 25, 81

SELF-INTEREST AND "THE GOOD OF SOCIETY"

Far from aligning any version of the kingdom of the world with the kingdom of God, kingdom-of-God participants must retain a healthy suspicion toward every version of the kingdom of the world – *especially their own* (for here it is most tempting to become idolatrous). After all, on the authority of God's Word, we know that however good a particular government may be by world standards, it is nevertheless strongly influenced by fallen principalities and powers.

> In our view of the world today, everything is topsy-turvy – just the opposite to what it is in God's sight.
>
> — A.E. Knoch

In fact, the kingdom-of-God citizen should know that, far from holding the ultimate answer to the world's problems, even the best versions of the kingdom of the world are part of the world's problem.

Every version of the kingdom of this world defends itself and advances its cause by rallying the *self-interests* of its citizens into a collective tribal force that makes each citizen willing to kill and be killed for what it believes to be *the good of society*. It survives and advances by uniting and motivating its subjects around their distinct collective identity, ideals, self-interest and desire for security – over and against any individuals or governments whose own tribal ideals, self-interest and desire for security might impinge on or threaten their own. To this end, every version of the kingdom of the world demonizes its enemies when necessary to generate the motivation to go to war and to convince those who must spill blood that their cause is righteous.

Gregory A. Boyd
The Myth of a Christian Nation (2005), pages 55-56

WHAT DO WE WAR AGAINST?

What about those of us who know "right division"? What should our response be to military service and the waging of war? To get an answer to this question we must go to the pen of the Apostle Paul.

> *Though we walk in the flesh, we do not war after the flesh (For the weapons of our warfare* **are not carnal,** *but mighty through God to the pulling down of strong holds)* (II Corinthians 10:3-4).

Paul very clearly states that the weapons of our warfare are not carnal, that is to say they are not physical. I cannot help but wonder every time I watch the news if the Body of Christ fully understands this important truth. I watch the world wage a war on terror with physical weapons trying to inflict a mortal blow on enemies who would try to destroy our way of life. Our weapons are not carnal; they are not those of the flesh, not such as the people of the world use. They are not such as are employed by conquerors; nor are they such as people in general rely on to advance their cause. We do not depend on eloquence, or talent, or learning, or wealth, or beauty, or any of the external aids on which the people of this world rely. They are not such as deriving advantage from any power inherent in themselves, or the weapons which can be mass-produced. Their strength is derived from God alone. But they are mighty through God. They are rendered mighty or powerful by the agency of God. They depend on Him for their efficacy. Paul has not here specified the weapons on which he relied; but he had before specified them so that there was no danger of mistake. The following verses state what these weapons are:

> *By pureness, by knowledge, by longsuffering, by kindness, by the Holy Spirit, by love unfeigned, by the Word of Truth, by the power of God, by the armor of righteousness on the right hand and on the left* (II Corinthians 6:6-7).

> The Creator is the sole responsible party for the final outcome.
>
> — Arthur P. Adams

Bill Petri
War and Grace (2006)

CHRIST VS. WAR

Christ says, *"Love your enemies;"*
    War says, "Hate them."

Christ says, *"Bless them who curse you;"*
    War says, "Curse them that curse you."

Christ says, *"Do good to them;"*
    War says, "Do them harm."

Christ says, *"Pray for them;"*
    War says, "Slay them."

Christ says, *"I am not come to destroy men's lives, but to save them;"*
> War says, "I am come to destroy men's lives."

Paul says, *"Overcome evil with good;"*
> War says, "Overcome evil with evil."

Paul says, *"If your enemy hungers, feed him;"*
> War says, "Starve him."

Paul says, *"If he thirsts, give him drink;"*
> War says, "Destroy his wells."

Paul says, *"We wrestle not against flesh and blood;"*
> War says, "We do wrestle against flesh and blood."

Daniel Vaniman (1835-1903)
Christ and War
Brethren Publishing House (1900)

What kind of government is the best? In school the children are taught that the form of government they are under is the best. ... All of the different forms of government, from anarchy to absolute despotism, are according to the purpose of God. They are all bad insofar as they are not subject to God ... [However] God does not make all authority bad now. He gives good rulers once in a while by way of change, because we need the contrasts ... [But] It is their failure that fulfills God's purpose.

A.E. Knoch (1874-1965)
Unsearchable Riches
Volume 36, 1945

Chapter 13

Influencing Governments

Christianity actively seeks to influence governments "for Christ." However, God has not called the believer to "influence" governments. Rather, our sphere of divine influence is on the individual level: it is about personal relationships. We do not bring divine light for the purpose of brightening up the *"jurisdiction of darkness,"* but to contrast its darkness.

> *In the midst of a crooked and perverse nation, among whom you shine as lights in the world* (Philippians 2:15).

Take Paul in Rome, for instance. He was given by God the opportunity to have influence with Caesar's relatives. This influence was not an earthly political influence, but a heavenly one – transforming some of them to saints.

> *All the saints salute you, chiefly they who are of Caesar's household* (Philippians 4:22).

Those in the Body of Christ are *"neither Jew nor Gentile."* *"Gentile"* is, of course, translated from the same Greek word, *ethnos,* that is also rendered *"nations."* Believers are no longer a part of the *"nations"* (*i.e., "neither Jew nor Gentile"*), but a *"new creation"* (II Corinthians 5:17), the *"one new man"* (Ephesians 2:15). For the Body of Christ there is no "us" and "them" of nationalism; we are no longer American or Canadian, Virginian or Pennsylvanian, Northerner or Southerner, Democrat or Republican, Conservative or Liberal, for we, *"from now on, are acquainted with no one according to flesh"* (II Corinthians 5:16, *CLNT*).

Our brother Frank Kujawa fittingly puts it this way:

> Terrestrial rule is not for us. Our realm is in the heavens.
>
> — A. E. Knoch

Galatians 3 tells us that we are *"neither Jew nor Gentile ..."* So what are we? A NEW creature in Christ! We *new* creatures no longer draw lines in the sand. All lines are divisions that cause conflicts. Conflicts can wound another emotionally, and ultimately lead to physical wounds, death and wars. A person in conflict is not free.

Think of it this way: Paul tells us that we are no longer Gentiles. During his time a Gentile was any nationality other than a Jew. So, in essence Paul tells us that we are "no longer of any nationality." Nations and national leaders are for those who do not know the Truth. The Truth has set us free.

Paul's instructions related to human governments are limited to our attitude and responsibility toward those who are in authority. There is no record of his instruction toward our influencing, changing or revolutionizing nations. Our instructions are:

I exhort therefore, that, first of all, supplications, prayers, intercessions and giving of thanks be made for all men; for kings, and for all who are in authority; that we may lead a quiet and peaceable life in all godliness and honesty (I Timothy 2:1-2).

Paul was not politically active. Take the issue of slavery, for example. We do not have any record of Paul advocating, nor campaigning for its abolition. *This* was NOT *his* agenda. He was *not* an activist for social and political change. However horrible slavery may have been, and no matter how honorable the cause of abolition may have been, such advocacy was actually below his *"high calling of God in Christ Jesus"* (Philippians 3:14). He had a celestial agenda toward which he pressed, with lesser causes left to lesser callings.

Paul did not lecture governments and leaders on the evils of slavery (or any other cause). Instead, remarkably, he instructed the slaves and their masters directly:

Servants, be obedient to them who are your masters according to the flesh, with fear and trembling, in singleness of your heart, as to Christ; not

> God ushered evil into the world and He will escort it out when it has accomplished His purpose.
>
> — Frank Neil Pohorlak

with eye-service, as men-pleasers; but as the servants of Christ, doing the will of God from the heart; with good will doing service, as to the Lord, and not to men: Knowing that whatever good thing any man does, the same he shall receive of the Lord, whether he is bond or free. And, you masters, do the same things to them,

*forbearing threatening: knowing that your Master also
is in heaven; neither is there respect of persons with Him*
(Ephesians 6:5-9).

This passage truly is remarkable, when you stop and think
about it; and it is only one example of Paul's focus. Paul was
the celestial apostle, writing to a celestial people, about their
celestial calling and citizenship. He instructs them concerning the details of living here on foreign soil as ambassadors
of their homeland, for, truly, we have been delivered *"... from
the dominion of darkness"* and have been *"transferred ... into
the Kingdom of His dear Son"* (Colossians 1:13), having Him
as our *"only Potentate"* (*"Ruler,"* Darby Translation, I Timothy 6:15), with *"our politics [politeuma] being in heaven; from
where also we look for the Savior, the Lord Jesus Christ"* (Philippians 3:20). Do not settle for less.

The eras of the nations, in which we live, bring us to the culmination and climax of man's misrule. ... There is a well-known work, "The Decline and Fall of the Roman Empire," which traces the descent of one of the great nations. Yet Rome was just a sample of all the rest. All other nations more or less conform to this pattern.

A.E. Knoch (1874-1965)
Unsearchable Riches
Volume 38, 1947

Chapter 14

Taxation and Other Concerns

PAUL AND TAXATION

Christians are not parasites enjoying the benefits of highways, mail service, etc. without helping to pay for them. Neither are we responsible for the way the government uses our tax money any more than we are responsible for the way the airlines or the grocer use the money we pay for service. There are no strings attached to the commands of Romans 13:6-7.

Pay tribute also ... Render therefore to all their dues: tribute to whom tribute is due; custom to whom custom; fear to whom fear; honor to whom honor.

JESUS AND ROMAN TAXATION

Before we consider the significance of what we are about to read from the Gospel According to Luke, it would do us well to realize that Romans were the *usurpers* of the government given to the nation of Israel. They were their oppressors and foreign enemies. If any group of people *ever* had an argument for not paying taxes, surely it was the Jews. They were God's nation. A Gentile nation was suppressing them.

Jesus was questioned concerning paying tribute (*i.e.*, taxes) to Caesar. His response can be found in all of the synoptic Gospels:

> *"Is it lawful for us to give tribute to Caesar, or not?" But He perceived their craftiness, and said to them, "Why tempt me? Show me a penny. Whose image and super-scription does it have?" They answered and said, "Cae-sar's." And He said to them, "Render therefore to Caesar the things which are Caesar's, and to God the things which are God's"* (Luke 20:22-26; *cf.* Matthew 22; Mark 12).

Tax Issues Are *Irrelevant* – Pay Them

Jesus made a case for the payment of taxes – no exceptions given.

Similarly, we live under, submit to and enjoy the benefits of a monetary system (however corrupt) whose image and sub-scription is that of a Gentile (*i.e.*, *heathen*) nation. Shall we refuse to do less than Christ taught?

In fact, Jesus made an even stronger appeal for the payment of taxes in Matthew 17:24-27. In this passage, Jesus com-pletely sets aside any issue of *legal* obligation to pay taxes and teaches that there is a *greater* issue at hand.

> *When they had come to Capernaum, they who received tribute money came to Peter and said, "Does your Mas-ter pay tribute?" He said, "Yes." And when he had come into the house, Jesus prevented him, saying, "What do you think, Simon? Of whom do the kings of the earth take custom or tribute? Of their own children, or of strangers?" Peter sad to Him, "Of strangers." Jesus said to him, "Then are the children free. **Nevertheless,** lest we should offend them, go to the sea, and cast a hook,*

and take up the fish that first comes up; and when you have opened his mouth, you will find a piece of money: take that, and give to them for you and Me."

Christ's message was *offensive* enough without adding further offense in an *irrelevant issue*. Paul repeats this principle:

Give none offence, neither to the Jews, nor to the nations, nor to the church of God (I Corinthians 10:32).

C.R. Stam (1909-2003) writes concerning the subject of taxation,

Those who, in our day, complain of corrupt government and assume the prerogative to decide whether or not they should pay taxes should reflect that Paul lived under the wicked Nero[1] and his corrupt administration, and *he* bids us to pay our taxes (Romans 13:6-7), and our Lord, also living under pagan Rome, taught His disciples to pay their taxes (Matthew 22:16-21; 17:24-27). This is *God's Word* on the matter.[2]

Paul's Teaching Is for the Body of Christ

For the grace of God that brings salvation has appeared to all men, teaching us that, denying ungodliness and worldly lusts ... (Titus 2:11-12).

---

1. "The Roman government ... deified Nero, ran a welfare state, and sponsored many pagan practices. Rome certainly did not use its tax money as Christians would desire. The tax-collectors of Jesus' time, who usually were paid no salary but rather became rich by overcharging and cheating people, certainly did not employ fair methods of taxation. Yet Jesus and Paul both spoke very clearly on the subject: the Christian ought to pay his taxes." – Eidsmor, p. 37.
2. Cornelius R. Stam, *Commentary on the Epistle of Paul to the Romans* (Chicago: Berean Bible Society, 1981), p. 310.

The teachings of Paul are clearly reserved for the saints. Grace teaching (*i.e.,* grace motivated living) is taught *only* to the believer. There is no unbeliever enrolled in grace's school. The religious system offers only a cheap imitation (*cf.,* II Timothy 3:5). It tries to reform the conduct of the world; but the world is simply being who they are in Adam. What they need is *Good News!*

Since Paul's instructions are for *us,* then how would we apply the following verses to the situation of war?

> *Though we walk in the flesh, we do not war after the flesh: (For the weapons of our warfare are not carnal, but mighty through God to the pulling down of strong holds)* (II Corinthians 10:3-4).

> *Put on the whole armor of God, that you may be able to stand against the wiles of the devil. For we wrestle not against flesh and blood, but against principalities, against powers, against the rulers of the darkness of this world, against spiritual wickedness in heavenly places* (Ephesians 6:11-12).

> *Therefore if your enemy hungers, feed him; if he thirsts, give him drink: for in so doing you will heap coals of fire on his head* (Romans 12:20).

Think how *contrary* these verses are to killing another man in battle. Is this our divine purpose? Should we be involved in the slaughter of the heathen? Is this the role to which God has called us? Or, should we be entreating them to *"be reconciled to God"* with the *"good news of the Happy God"*?

What if we, while active participants in a war, killed a man who was a fellow-believer? Are we to take up arms against fellow-members of Christ's Body for some supposed national "good"? Could such a thing happen? Didn't it happen during the American *Civil War*? "Brother against brother," not only in the biological sense, but also in the spiritual as well? Serious consideration should be given to this issue before the believer *patriotically* heads off to war.

Or, how would we apply the following verse to a political campaign?

> *To speak evil of no man, to be no brawlers, but gentle, showing all meekness to all men* (Titus 3:2).

Or, how would we apply this verse to a courtroom?[3]

> *Be kind to each other, tenderhearted, forgiving one another, even as God for Christ's sake has forgiven you* (Ephesians 4:32).

Or, how could you apply this verse to capital punishment?

Recompense to no man evil for evil ... (Romans 12:17).

The list could go on.

Are we to compartmentalize our lives – sacred life and secular life? Are we to turn "on" and "off" the life of Christ in us? Are we to follow the instructions of our Savior through Paul only when it is convenient?

Just how could we apply these verses to the contexts that we have suggested? Simply put, I do not see how we can. They will not work! We are operating in a completely *different* realm!

Should we attempt to "Christianize" nationalism? Maybe we should ask those who lived in the fourth century under

---

3. See Appendix 3: *Jury Duty.*

the "Christian" Constantine; or those who lived in the Dark Ages under Roman Catholicism; or those who lived in John Calvin's "Christian" Geneva;[4] or, yes, even those living in the Puritan colony of Massachusetts.[5]

The *"religious* right" are no more the friends of Paul's gospel than the "non-religious left."[6] Remember that the tree in the garden was the tree of the knowledge of *good* and evil! Beware of human *good*, as well as human evil!

Lloyd Hartzler remarks,

> The state could not operate effectively by the principles of New Testament ethics. Suppose law officers would attempt to use the ethics of grace in handling thieves, murderers or rapists?[7]

Also, we might ask, could the believer operate within the system of government by the principles of Pauline truth?

Listen to what John Saunders has to say about our *identification* with human government:

---

4. See Appendix 2: *John Calvin's Geneva*
5. "The Puritans did not flee religious persecution in settling America but para-doxically established it. The historian Miller rightly declared: 'The government of Massachusetts, and of Connecticut as well, was a dictatorship, and never pretended to be anything else; it was a dictatorship, not of a single tyrant, or of an economic class, or of a political faction, but of the holy and regenerate.' He further states, 'They maintained here precisely what they maintained in England, and if they exiled, fined, jailed, whipped, or hanged those who disagreed with them in New England, they would have done the same thing in England could they have secured the power.'" – Laurence M. Vance, *The Other Side of Calvinism* (Pensacola: Vance Publications, 1991), p. 9.
6. The religious right is filled with those who are being motivated by *dominion* and *reconstruction* theology. They *appear* to be fighting the good fight, but are you aware of the teachings and goals of those who hold such views? If you were you might be shocked! If those who held these views had control they would *not* be your friend. For a look at these teachings, from the very works of their own leaders, see *Vengeance Is Ours,* by Albert James Dager (Redmond, WA: Sword Publishers, 1990).
7. Lloyd Hartzler, *The Christian and the State*, p. 7.

In reality, American Christians, Russian Christians – all Christians – have been called to live as strangers and aliens even in the lands of our birth (II Corinthians 6:16-18) …

When the enemy can get the Lord's people to wrestle with flesh and blood, his objective is accomplished, because he has disarmed the church. How foolish we are to lay down our divinely powerful weapons of the Spirit in favor of the puny weapons of mere men. If we take our eyes off of our Head, the Lord Jesus, and put our trust in human institutions and the arm of the flesh, we have lost the battle (even if it seems momentarily that we have won), and what is worse, we have lost our testimony.

> *We hold these truths to be self-evident, that all men are endowed by their Creator with certain inalienable rights, among which are the right to life, liberty, and the pursuit of happiness.*

These are attractive, high-sounding words to be sure, but they do not have one whit of scriptural backing. The unbeliever who penned them certainly did not get his ideas from the Scriptures. That is why he said it was *"self-evident"* – in other words, it sounded like a good idea to him. And from that shaky foundation, we who live in America today are so addicted to our idols of freedom and materialism that we have incorporated them right into the church and our practice of Christianity.

"Life, liberty, and the pursuit of happiness" may square well with the Christianity practiced by the Crusaders in the Middle Ages, but it certainly has nothing in common with the kingdom of which our Lord is the King …

Don't get me wrong. I prefer living in a free society to the alternative. But if my lust for freedom blinds me to the kingdoms of this world, then it would be better to live under tyranny than to sell my birthright in Christ for the materialistic licentiousness of democratic capitalism. Living in America makes us love the world, because here, we have the very best of it. Somehow we Christians tell ourselves that *our* country, above all others, is ordained by God and is called to be a special nation before Him. This idea is about as valid as the self-evidency proposition.

The result of all of this is that most of the Christians in America find themselves *identifying* with the world system and, in fact, wedded to it. We are called to be strangers and aliens even in the land of our birth.

Why do we always say "*we*" when referring to our country? God has transported us out of the kingdom of darkness and into the kingdom of His marvelous light. Yet the largest movement of Christians in America today is to seize control of the government and its vital institutions so that we may "once again" have a Christian nation. This nation is about as Christian as a football game at which the spectators sober up for a few moments of silence while some clergyman offers the invocation. What the enemy has been unable to do through centuries of persecution, he has managed to do to the church in America by dissipation.

I am not at all unaware of the numerous books written about the founding of America and our "*special*" relationship to God and our "*holy*" heritage. The problem is that not one bit of this thinking and rationale can be squared with the Scriptures. Nowhere has the Lord instructed His people to go out and found a nation based on Bible principles or anything else. The fact that men have done such things in the name of God is no assurance at all that He has desired it any more than He stood with Herod when he "beautified" the temple. We Americans don't understand this because, rooted deep in our hearts, is the delusion that God is ever so grateful to anyone who will launch some high-minded scheme – if they will only proclaim they are doing it in His Name."[8]

8. John Saunders, *The Tiger Is Dead*, (Memphis: Guardian Books, 1989) pp. 74-79.

"Government by the People." It is of major importance that the people as a whole be given an opportunity to govern themselves. Without this, God's great demonstration of human impotence would be far from convincing. Not only that, but it is very helpful to have so many varieties and gradations of popular rule.

A.E. Knoch (1874-1965)
Unsearchable Riches
Volume 38, 1947

Chapter 15

Λuϲhoriϲy, Suϐmission and Oϐedience

Submission to Foreign Authorities

*J*f we take our passports and visit a foreign country, we should always be on our best behavior while there. Just because believers are citizens of heaven, it does not mean that they should disregard the authorities of the foreign county in which they temporarily reside.

In Christ there is *"neither bond nor free"* (Galatians 3:28). Even so, Paul instructs servants to *"be obedient to their own masters"* (Titus 2:9). In Christ there is *"neither male nor female"* (Galatians 3:28), but Paul still teaches wives to *"submit yourselves to your own husbands"* (Ephesians 5:22). In Christ we are celestial citizens, but Paul nevertheless insists that we be in submission to governmental authorities (Romans 13:1-7; Titus 3:1; *cf.* I Peter 2:13-14).

The Meaning of Authority

Noah Webster defines authority as "power, or right to command or act." It should be evident to the believer that it is God Himself Who is *the* Authority of the universe. In fact, it is His authority that is the only *natural* and *absolute* authority. *All* other authority in the universe is *delegated* and *derived* from Him.

When God delegates authority it is a very serious matter for the ones with whom it is vested, and to the ones in submission towards it. All who have been delegated with authority by God are servants of God, whether that authority is in the home (Ephesians 5:22-6:3; Colossians 3:18-22), government (Romans 13:1-7; Titus 3:1; I Peter 2:13-14), or employment (Ephesians 6:5-7; I Timothy 6:1; Titus 2:9-10). Those with delegated authority from God are *accountable to Him* for that authority.

THE ONLY PROPER RESPONSE TO AUTHORITY

The primary response toward authority is *submission*. It is authority's counterpart. Improper attitudes toward authority are an affront to the source of all authority – God Himself.

Submission has become a repulsive term in our day. In the minds of many it often has the connotation of inferiority, weakness, inequality, or even slavery and oppression. However, submission primarily describes the way a relationship is ordered, structured and conducted. Submission does not mean that one is less important or inferior. It is very important that we have a clear understanding that submission is *not* an issue of "superiority," but simply one of "function."

WHAT SUBMISSION IS

The Greek word for submit is *hupotasso* (*hupo* = under; and *tasso* = set in order). Submission is the act of yielding to the authority of another. It is the opposite of resistance. As in the case of the traffic sign, yielding is the act of "giving way" or "allowing another the right-of-way."

TRUE SUBMISSION AS MANIFEST IN CHRIST

[Jesus Christ] *went down with them* [Joseph and Mary], *and came to Nazareth, and was **subject** to them* (Luke 2:51).

The nature of submission can be seen clearly here in this verse. Christ *Himself* was under submission. Does this mean that He was inferior to Joseph and Mary? *No!* Were they *better* than He? *ABSOLUTELY NOT!* Let us state it once more: delegated authority, and submission to it, have *nothing* to do with inferiority and superiority, but function!

Submission is the God-ordained way whereby individuals may relate to each other and properly and orderly channel all of their actions, abilities, ideas, wisdom, talents, education, etc.

More than anything else, submission is an *attitude* of the heart towards authority. As we have seen from the last passage, even Christ, while on earth, submitted to divinely appointed authority.

THE RELATIONSHIP BETWEEN ABSOLUTE SUBMISSION AND RELATIVE OBEDIENCE

Submission and obedience must not be confused.[1] Submission primarily has to do with *attitude*. Obedience, on the other hand, has to do chiefly with *compliance* to *authority* (*i.e.*, actions).

As Watchman Nee points out,

When *delegated* authority (men who represent God's authority) and *direct* authority (God Himself) are in con-

---

1. "Submission ... should not be confused with obedience." Ceslas Spicq, *Theological Lexicon of the New Testament,* Volume 3, p. 424.

flict, one can render submission but not obedience to the delegated authority.[2]

COMPLEXITY OF OBEDIENCE

Obedience is often complicated by complex multi-tiered governments that are prevalent in Western societies.

For example, in the United States one has local, county, state and federal statutes and authorities, not to mention international ones such as those of the United Nations. These statutes or authorities can't always be in harmony. How could they be, with hundreds of millions of laws on the books, literally growing daily, and millions of government agents?

There is also the possible conflict of government documents with the personal directives by authorized government representatives. What if an individual (such as a President, a Governor, an administrator, a police officer, etc.) or a group of individuals (such as the federal or a state congress, a bureau, a committee, a council, a board, etc.) who have been vested with authority require actions contrary to government documents (such as the United States Constitution, a state constitution, the Bill of Rights, etc.)?

We are definitely *not* talking about mere hypothetical situations here. *Absolute* obedience to human authorities is an impossibility at times. As one source states,

> There are so many criminal laws, the odds of no one breaking one in a lifetime are so astronomical, it would make DNA odds look like simple math.[3]

If someone advocates *absolute* obedience to all human au-

---

2. Watchman Nee, *Spiritual Authority*, p. 107.
3. Answers.com, Answers Corporation.

thorities, when such authorities are at variance with each other, what method can be clearly shown from the pages of Scripture to resolve such a conflict?

No Other God Before Me

Those who are acquainted with the Scriptures know that the word "god"[4] is a broad-based word – it is the title of a magistrate. When we use it with an upper case "G" we refer to the *supreme* Magistrate – "God." When it is used with a lower case "g" it is a reference to an *inferior* magistrate – one *beneath* "God." For this reason, God gave the commandment to Israel,

*You shall have no other gods **before** Me* (Exodus 20:3).

The issue is not that Israel couldn't have any other "gods" they honored, revered or obeyed. The issue was that there could be none *before* Him. We see this stressed in the *Concordant Literal Old Testament* as,

*There shall not come to be other elohim for you in **preference** to Me.*

He and He alone was to be Israel's "God" with a capital "G." He of course delegated among them those who would have the authority of being *lower* magistrates.

You are gods; and all of you are children of the Most High (Psalm 82:6).

---

4. **HEBREW:** *elohiym* (Stong's #430 – gods in the ordinary sense; but specifically used of the supreme God; occasionally applied by way of deference to *magistrates;* and sometimes as a superlative). **GREEK:** *theos* (Strong's #2316 – a deity, especially [but not exclusively] the supreme Divinity; figuratively, a *magistrate*).

THE DIVINE CHAIN-OF-COMMAND

We learn a simple principle in all of this. Though there are other magistrates (*i.e.,* "*gods*") on the earth, none of them are to occupy a place *before* Him, the Supreme Magistrate – "*God*." Therefore, when there is a direct conflict (ordained by God, of course!) between a *lower* magistrate and the *Highest* Magistrate, we will defer to the Highest and obey Him, even if it means disobeying the lower one. They may be a "god," but they are not *the* "God." God alone is to occupy our *highest* allegiance, worship and obedience. *All* other "gods" are *subordinate* to Him. Therefore, if God's revealed will for the believer runs contrary to the will of earthly authorities, it is because Father desires a testimony of faith to be given by His chosen ones, and a demonstration of man's folly to be made in contrast with His wisdom and supremacy.

SUBMISSION IS ABSOLUTE, OBEDIENCE IS RELATIVE

Though submission to earthly authorities is *clearly* taught in Scriptures, some advocate that they also demand *absolute obedience* as well. Such is not the case.

The main passages usually used to defend such a position are Romans 13:1-7; Titus 3:1; and I Peter 2:13-14. In all three passages the issue is "*submission*" not "*obedience.*"

> *Let every soul be* **subject** *... Be* **subject** (Romans 13:1, 5).

> *Be* **subject** (Titus 3:1)

> *Be* **subject** (I Peter 2:13).

In each case above, the word "*subject*" is the Greek word *hupotasso.* As noted earlier, it is a compound word: *hupo,* meaning "under;" and *tasso*, meaning "set in order" – thus, "to set in order under."

Here are a few resources regarding *hupotasso:*

> UNDER-SET (*Concordant Keyword Concordance*).

> To subordinate (James Strong #5293).

> To arrange under (Joseph Thayer).

> Primarily a military term, to rank under (W.E. Vine).

> To set in array under (Robert Young).

> To place in order, to place under in orderly fashion (Spiros Zodhiates).

Hupotasso denotes order and structure. As one lexicon states,

> It means first of all accepting the exact place God has assigned, keeping one's rank in this or that society.[5]

Therefore, the usage of *hupotasso* in the Greek Scriptures correctly relates to submission, *not* to obedience. Let's consider some of the other relationships that *hupotasso* describes. In Romans 13 *hupotasso* is in the middle voice,[6] just as it is in all of these following passages:

> Believers' submission to each other (Ephesians 5:21).

---

5. Ceslas Spicq, *Theological Lexicon of the New Testament,* Volume 3, page 426.
6. "In the middle voice the subject is affected, more or less, by the action" (*Concordant Keyword Concordance*); meaning, in the case of *hupotasso,* to *"place oneself in submission."* —Spiros Zodhiates, *The Complete Word-study Dictionary: New Testament*).

Wives' submission to husbands (Ephesians 5:22; Colossians 3:18; Titus 2:5; I Peter 3:1, 5).

Servants' submission to masters (Titus 2:9; I Peter 2:18).

In each of these cases above, *hupotasso* is describing the way a certain relationship is ordered, or structured. There is to be a submissive spirit of honor, respect and reverence; *but,* would one seriously suggest that any of these others should include *absolute* obedience?

While believers should submit to each other, wives to husbands, and servants to masters, does this somehow mean that believers should *absolutely obey* each other, that wives should *absolutely obey* their husbands, and that servants should *absolutely obey* their masters – each without any exceptions? CERTAINLY NOT!

If a husband asks his wife to kill their children, should she obey?

Someone may object that this is just a hypothetical question, but it is not. There *are* evil men, waxing worse and worse (II Timothy 3:13), who hold authority at all of the levels of submission (*hupotasso*): there *are* evil magistrates, evil husbands and evil masters.

Contrary to what many believe and teach, there is no such thing as *absolute obedience* when it comes to human authority. Such obedience *always* has its limitations. There are no other "gods" *before* "God."

We ought to obey God rather than men (Acts 5:29).

We are to honor and respect those in authority, as they are "God's ministers." We should be subject to them. However, while a heart attitude of submission to human authority is absolute, obedience is not.

When the dictates of the state conflict with the clear teachings of Scripture, another biblical principle takes precedence:

Comments by Others on the Nature of Romans 13 as Related to Absolute Obedience

"Let every soul be subject" has been misunderstood by many, for it is not said, "Let every soul be obedient," and there is a difference.[7]

Paul does not deal here with the problem of what the Christian must do when the state authorities command him to preform acts which are in contradiction to his loyalty to Jesus Christ.[8]

There is a point surely beyond which we must render no obedience either to rulers or anyone else except God. If they were to demand of us what is due only to God – worship, for instance, as in the case of Daniel or his three friends – we must firmly refuse.[9]

When the dictates of the state conflict with the clear teachings of Scripture, another biblical principle took precedence: *"We ought to obey God rather than man"* (Acts 5:29). For this very reason Christians throughout history have fled homelands and have even forfeited their lives.[10]

7. R.E. Rhoades, *The Apostle Paul's Letter to the Romans*, p. 286.
8. James D. Smart, *Doorway to a New Age: A Study of Paul's Letter to the Romans*, p. 161.
9. L. M. Grant, *Comments on the Book of Romans*, p. 134.
10. Thoralf Gilbrant, *The New Testament Greek-English Dictionary*, volume 16, page 391.

While the believer may not agree with the government philosophy or politics of his nation, he is to be a good citizen of it. So long as a law does not violate his conscience before God, the Christian should obey it. Even if he defies such a law, he should be prepared and willing to endure the consequences of his allegiance to God.[11]

Jesus set a precedent in this matter, for although His words, *"Render to Ceaser the things that are Caesar's, and to God the things that are God's"* (Mark 12:17), were spoken with reference to the payment of tribute, they express a principle of more general application. ... When Caesar claims divine honors, the Christians' answer must be "No." ... Christians will voice their "No" to Caesar's unauthorized demands the more effectively if they have shown themselves ready to say "Yes" to all of his authorized demands.[12]

One must not disobey conscience in submitting to civil government. Without being a rebel he can refuse to do what he regards as wrong, but he must patiently endure the penalty.[13]

The rights of conscience are sacred and may never be infringed by the civil magistrate. God alone is Lord of conscience. ... That this is the true doctrine of Scripture is evident from the example of Daniel, Shadrach, Meshech and Abednego, and of the Apostles themselves, who openly proclaimed, *"We ought to obey God rather than men"* (Acts 5:29).[14]

The obedience which the Scriptures command us to ren-

---

11. Hershel H. Hobbs, *Romans: A Verse by Verse Study*, p. 153.
12. F.F. Bruce, *The Epistle to the Romans*, pp. 233, 234.
13. Charles R. Erdman, *The Epistle of Paul to the Romans*, p. 152.
14. William S. Plumer, *Commentary on Romans*, p. 589.

der to our rulers is not unlimited; there are cases in which disobedience is a duty.[15]

SCRIPTURAL EXAMPLES OF THE DISOBEDIENCE OF FAITH

We are familiar with the scriptural phrase *"obedience of faith,"* but there are many honorable examples in Scripture of the *disobedience of faith.*

It is quite possible to submit oneself to authority *and* at the same time be disobedient to some specific command. There is widespread Scripture testimony for believers' disobedience to earthly authorities as an extreme expression of their faith. We will note a few.

The Hebrew Midwives (Exodus 1:15-22)

The King of Egypt required the midwives to kill the male children born under their care. Shiphrah and Puah refused and, *"did not as the King of Egypt commanded them, but saved the male children alive. ... Therefore God dealt well with the midwives."*

Rahab (Joshua 2)

The King of Jericho directed Rahab to deliver the spies of Israel to him. She directly disobeyed the command, hiding them and helping them to escape. For the act of faith's disobedience, she is honored in Hebrews' Hall of Faith.

By faith the harlot Rahab perished not with them who believed not, when she had received the spies with peace (Hebrews 11:31) *and sent them out another way* (James 2:25).

---

15. Charles Hodge, cited by William S. Plumer, *Commentary on Romans*, page 589.

The Soldiers of Israel (I Samuel 14:24-30; 43-45)

The soldiers of Israel disobeyed the King, refusing to kill innocent Jonathan.

Obadiah (I Kings 18:4, 13-15)

When Queen Jezebel was killing God's prophets, Obadiah hid and protected a hundred of them.

The "Three Hebrew Children" (Daniel 3:1-7; 12-18).

Shadrach, Meshach and Abednego refused to comply with King Nebuchadnezzar's command to worship the golden image that he had erected.

Daniel (6:6-11, 16-28)

Daniel disobeyed King Nebuchadnezzar's thirty-day ban on prayer to God.

The Wise Men (Matthew 2:8, 12)

The Magi disobeyed the command of King Herod. Interestingly, it was God *Himself* Who instructed them to disobey. Herod told them to do one thing, God told them to do another. The wise men disobeyed Herod and obeyed God.

When those in human authority issue decrees contrary to those of God, it is clearly God, rather than man, that should be obeyed.

Peter and John (Acts 4:1-21; Acts 5:17-18; 26-29).

When the rulers of Israel (4:5, 8) decreed that Peter and John cease their teaching (4:18), they responded,

> *Whether it is right in the sight of God to listen to you*
> *more than to God, you decide. For we cannot but speak*
> *the things which we have seen and heard* (Acts 4:19-20).

Some assert that the Apostles were only disobeying *religious* mandates, not governmental ones. Those attempting to make such a distinction do not understand the nature of Israel, nor her status under the jurisdiction of Rome. Israel was functioning as a religious-political entity, under the authority of the Roman Empire. These rulers of Israel before whom Peter and John were summoned were operating under Roman authority. This is why, when their decrees were violated, they had the authority to arrest the Apostles and place them in prison (5:18).

This is the same type of religious-political union that believers faced throughout the Dark Ages.

When Martin Luther appeared before the *Diet of Worms,* he faced the civil-ecclesiastical authority. When he refused to recant he defied the law. When ask by the Inquisitor, "Doest thou admit that these books are written by thee? Wilt thou retract these books and their contents, or doest thou persist in the things thou hast advanced?" he responded,

> Unless I can be convicted of error by the Holy Scripture, I
> neither can nor dare retract anything, for my conscience
> is held captive by God's Word. Here I stand, I can do not
> otherwise; so God help me. Amen.

Paul Our Apostle

For some, there seems to be quite a disconnect between what they suggest is Paul's teaching of absolute obedience and his straightforward life of civil disobedience. Surely, if *anyone* knew the meaning of Romans 13:1-7 and Titus 3:1, it would have been their author, Paul. He obviously did not believe that they sanctioned some supposed *absolute obedience* to earthly magistrates. Paul's was a long story of run-ins with the law. He was repeatedly imprisoned and eventually executed by civil authorities.

PAUL THE CRIMINAL

Remember that Jesus Christ of the seed of David was raised from the dead according to my gospel: wherein I suffer trouble, as an evil doer, even to bonds (II Timothy 2:8-9).

Early in Paul's ministry he was assailed by trumped-up charges; but over time, as the attitude of the government toward him and his message grew intolerant, his ministry was made illegal and he was imprisoned as an *"evil doer."*

This phrase *"evil doer"* is a translation of the Greek word *kakourgos,* which James Strong (#2557) defines as "a criminal." Both Weymouth and Moffatt render it *"criminal"* in their translations. At last, Paul suffered evil, *"as a criminal."*

It was Paul's distinct *"my gospel"* that had steered him into his troubles with authorities. Note that it was, *"my gospel: **wherein I suffer trouble."***

At the time of his writing of II Timothy, Paul was imprisoned under the great persecution of Nero. Only state-approved religions were accepted and allowed to practice legally under Roman authority. At first, Paul's ministry was allowed under the assumed auspices of Judaism, but as His revelations from God continued to show that they were distinct and separate, his message and ministry became illegal.

So, it was the very message of Paul that caused his troubles. Now Paul, even with his privileged Roman citizenship, was imprisoned and suffered execution *"as a criminal."* Yet, while disobedient, he always exuded a spirit of submission with respect, honor and non-resistance. His was a godly attitude of subjection, while giving a testimony of the *disobedience of faith.*

RELIGIO ILLICITA

Christianity was publicly declared to be *illegal* by Rome. The more that Paul preached the distinction of his gospel, the more he distanced himself from Judaism, the more he lost his "legal" umbrella of *"religious* freedom." Every time Paul taught his mystery gospel, he assured another nail for his coffin. Paul's gospel was illegal!

Merrill C. Tenney (1904-1985) describes for us the situation in which Paul found himself:

> [Cornelius] Tacitus [56-117], writing of the times of Nero, calls Christians "enemies of the human race" (*Annals* xv. 44).

> Judaism was a *religio licita* [legal religion], and the Christians, as a sect of Judaism, enjoyed the privilege of protection ... [But when] they were openly separated from Judaism [by the distinct ministry of Paul] they became a *religio illicita* [illegal religion], with no official standing, nor even the right to exist ... They were liable to prosecution if the magistrates found a plausible excuse for harassing them, and they could claim no immunity or redress.[16]

Robert H. Gundry also writes,

> The Roman government still regarded Christianity as a branch of Judaism and therefore a *religio licita* (legal reli-

---

16. Merrill C. Tenney, *Exploring New Testament Culture: A Handbook of New Testament Times,* pp. 125, 303.

gion). The Roman policy was to grant freedom to all existing religions in the empire, but to ban new religions for fear of the social turmoil caused by their invasion. Only at a later date, when the Romans realized that Christianity was distinct from Judaism, did they ban Christianity as a *religio illicita* (illegal religion).[17]

There are rare occasions when some believers, in some societies, in some generations, are required by their own conscience to disobey earthly magistrates. This action should never be taken lightly – it is a serious matter for which the believer's faith could be severely tested by those who *bear not the sword in vain.*

There are, however, worse things than disobedience to man. Though the believer in such situations should always do everything within their power to be peaceful, kind, gentle and cooperative – showing all due honor and respect to the magistrates – the ultimate Magistrate is God, to Whom is due *absolute* obedience.

> We are called to the ministry of conciliation and must not oppose those whom God has been pleased to put over us in any matter *which does not violate our conscience.*
>
> *Unsearchable Riches*
> Volume 10, 1918

As with the many examples given earlier, where believers have faced the authorities for their terrestrial disobedience, there can be an opportunity for an unparalleled testimony for God. There is something extremely powerful about the humble, non-resistant presence of faith that, in clear conscience before God, can look a magistrate directly, unashamedly in the eyes and with boldness declare such words as these:

---

17. Robert H. Gundry, *A Survey of the New Testament* (1978), p. 236.

Our God Whom we serve is able to deliver us from the burning fiery furnace ... But if not, be it known to you, O King, that we will not serve your gods (Daniel 3:17-18).

Whether it is right in the sight of God to listen to you more than to God, you judge; for we cannot but speak the things which we have seen and heard (Acts 4:19-20).

We ought to obey God rather than men (Acts 5:29).

Unless I can be convicted of error by the Holy Scripture, I neither can nor dare retract anything, for my conscience is held captive by God's Word. Here I stand, I can do not otherwise; so God help me. Amen.

Men do not really make up their minds. They are made up for them. All are powerfully influenced by the spirit forces which can be neither seen nor felt, but which can be detected by their effect. The spirit of the times carries men on its current. ...

But a believer should not be caught in the current of the spirit which carries the sons of stubbornness to destruction. ... Our comprehension is no longer darkened, it is true, but all of the actual light which it has comes to us direct from God, by His spirit, through His Word.

A.E. Knoch (1874-1965)
The Problem of Evil
pages 109, 110

Chapter 16

Nationalists Want to Agitate Your Spirit!

Take a Deep Breath, and Relax in Father

Peace I leave with you. My peace I give to you: not as the world gives, give I to you. Let not your heart be troubled, neither let it be afraid (John 14:27).

To be spiritually minded is life and peace (Romans 8:6).

The peace of God, which passes all understanding, will keep your hearts and minds through Christ Jesus (Philippians 4:7).

Let the peace of God rule in your hearts (Colossians 3:15).

One of the greatest assets of the child of God is peace. It is the divine counterpart to grace. Thus, Paul repeats in each of his epistles, *"grace and peace."* This is not a religious cliché: it is our divine heritage as sons of God.

Peace is defined as:

Freedom from disturbance; tranquility (*Oxford Dictionary*).

Inner contentment; serenity (*American Heritage Dictionary*).

Freedom from disquieting or oppressive thoughts or emotions (*Merriam-Webster Dictionary*).

Calm and quiet; freedom from worry or annoyance (*Cambridge Dictionary*).

Freedom from agitation or disturbance by the passions, as from fear, terror, anger, anxiety or the like; quietness of mind; tranquility; calmness; quiet of conscience (*Webster's Original 1828*).

> Nothing can thwart or disarrange God's plans; there is no possibility of failure.
>
> — Arthur P. Adams

There surely is much uncertainty and turmoil in the world around us; but there is one thing that we need to remember: God is not *ruffled* by earthly events and details in the least. This is because He is God – and He is in sovereign control of *everything*. Simply put, this means that God is at peace – no wringing of His hands, no wiping of His brow – after all, Paul calls Him the *"God of peace"* (Romans 15:33; 16:20; Philippians 4:19; I Thessalonians 5:23).

There are two distinct scriptural spheres of divine peace: *"peace **with** God,"* and *"the peace **of** God."* We have *"peace **with** God"*

> God is demonstrating the futility of human government now.
>
> — A. E. Knoch

because of the work of our Lord Jesus Christ on Golgotha's tree. *All* enmity and strife between us and God has been permanently removed. Paul declared that Christ *"was delivered for our offences and was raised again for our justification,"* and that, *"therefore, being justified by faith,"* we, who once were estranged from God in our hearts and minds, enjoy *"peace **with** God through our Lord Jesus Christ"* (Romans 4:25; 5:1).

However, it is one thing to have *"peace **with** God,"* and quite another to have *"the peace **of** God."* It is our divinely-given privilege to enjoy not only *"peace **with** God,"* but *"the peace **of** God"* as well. In fact, Father desires that we be at rest *with Him* in every detail of life, enjoying His very Own unworried and tranquil spirit. We are to *let the **peace of God** rule in our hearts, i.e.,* to take charge of all of our cares, concerns and worries, the peace of His Own nature and character settling our hearts!

> *Let the peace of God settle[1] in your hearts* (Colossians 3:15).

The *"peace **of** God"* is your God-given possession; therefore, *don't let anyone or anything agitate your spirit!*

Who or what manages to get *under your skin* and causes you

---

1. *"Settle"* – Weymouth, Colossians 3:15.

to lose your peace? Are they *bigger* than Father? Do they in any way threaten His plan for you? Can they derail His purpose for you? Certainly not! If He *is* the God of the universe, then why allow your spirit to be agitated by others?

One area that seems to bring great agitation to many is that of nationalism. For all of my adult life I have seen professing believers allow their spirits to be agitated by social, political and economic pundits of nationalism and patriotism. For over four decades I have watched Christians surrender their God-given peace to these commercial agitators.

My first exposure to them was through such national personalities as Carl McIntire, Billy James Hargis, W.S. McBirnie, Dan Smoot, Willis Carto and Robert Welch.

A couple of generations have passed, but the stirring rhetoric continues. Their modern prophets include Bill Maher, Bill O'Reilly, James Carville, Rush Limbaugh, Sean Hannity, Glenn Beck, Jon Stewart, Neal Boortz and Michael Savage.

Don't let them agitate your spirit. Don't allow them to displace your peace.

> Knowing that God's hand is in everything, we can leave everything in God's hand.

Listen to Paul's wonderful words of encouragement to us,

Be anxious for nothing; *but in everything by prayer and supplication with thanksgiving let your requests be made known to God. And the peace of God, which passes all understanding, shall keep your hearts and minds through Christ Jesus* (Philippians 4:6-7).

While only those who know that they are at *"peace **with** God"* can know *"the peace **of** God,"* it does not follow, however, that all of those who know that they are at *"peace **with** God"* necessarily enjoy *"the peace **of** God."* Believers can enjoy *"the peace **of** God"* only as they practice Philippians 4:6 and turn every care over to His capable hands – all of our trials, all of our problems. As we follow these instructions, the promise which follows will certainly be fulfilled.

> He Who governed the world before I was born shall take care of it likewise when I am dead.
>
> — John Wesley

> *The peace of God, which passes all understanding, shall keep [*"guard,"* Rotherham; *"garrison,"* Weymouth] your hearts and minds through Christ Jesus (:7).*

God is *never* caught surprised. He knows *exactly* what He is doing. We can have complete confidence in Him because nothing is outside of His sovereign control. Therefore, we should not be overwhelmed and defeated by the adversities of life.

> *We know that **all things** work together for good to them who love God, to them who are the called according to His purpose (Romans 8:28).*

PEACE EVEN IN THE SPHERE OF NATIONALISM

> *Why do the nations rage? (Psalm 2:1; Acts 4:25).*

Why is man's life filled with such vanity; such futility, emptiness, barrenness, purposelessness and aimless frustration? Because he has been subjected so by his Creator.

The creature was made subject to vanity, not willingly, but by reason of Him Who has subjected the same in hope (Romans 8:20).

> There is not one problem in the universe that God does not have the answer to, because they all originated in Him.
>
> — John Essex

Life is vain when viewed apart from the sovereign, loving God Who is our Father. *"Vanity"* is the lot of man *"under the sun."* All areas of life illustrate and demonstrate the vanity of life apart from God (Ecclesiastes 1:2-8). Vanity is the purpose of *Phase One* of our existence.

I feel for those who face daily life apart from the knowledge that He *alone* is in complete control. Many live their daily lives without recognition of the stabilizing truth of the One Who *"works all things after the counsel of His Own will"* (Ephesians 1:11). They approach their day and struggle through it as the master of their own lives.

For those who live as though they were in charge of their lives, two of the hardest parts of the day are waking up in the morning and going to bed in the evening. In the mornings, days are greeted with uncertainty as thoughts of the "What if …" trials and challenges of the day press in on the mind and heart. There is a waking up to varying degrees of uneasiness, concern, apprehension, worry and anxiety – even at times to overwhelming fear, dread and depression. Feelings of inadequacy and uncertainty press in.

In the evenings, days are retired with the annoying "What if …" reflections of its happenings. There is second-guessing, regret and disappointment. Feelings of frustration, dissatisfaction and failure settle in – even at times shame, guilt and worthlessness.

After all, they see themselves as the lords of their own lives, the captains of their own ships and the masters of their own destiny. With this view comes but a recurring cycle of vanity.

Those of us who know Father as the great Planner and Director of our days have a completely different approach to our mornings and evenings – and the entire unfolding of our every minute of our day.

In the mornings, days can be greeted with the joy and excitement of knowing that *they* as well as ourselves are His. The uncertainties of the "What if ..." viewpoint are divinely transformed into the eager anticipation of seeing what God has planned for the day. We are able to awaken to the thrill of knowing that we will be witnesses of the unfolding of His detailed plan and purpose for our day. His presence presses in on our minds. There is an awaking to peace and joy as we know that our life, with all of its daily circumstances, is firmly in His hand and carried out by His capable direction. Our hearts are able to say, "Today we are on the great adventure of faith!"

> If "evil men shall wax worse" in the latter days, then why are we so amazed that it's happening?
>
> — André Sneidar

In the evenings, when the day is over, we can rest our heads on our pillows, and with surety and confidence regarding our day say, "This was the will of God." The "What if ..." reflections of its happenings are transformed into a place of peace and rest, knowing that the will of God was done, and who could have prevented it? The realization of our divine appointment is able to settle within our hearts and minds. After all, He is the Lord of our life, the Captain of our ship, the Master of our destiny.

> *He does according to His will in the army of heaven, and among the inhabitants of the earth: and none can restrain His hand* (Daniel 4:35).

The *"peace of God"* that we possess has nothing to do with family, neighborhood, civil, social or national peace. The issue is that *our hearts* are aligned with God and His purpose, thus bringing quietness and peace to our hearts and to the very disposition of our lives.

No matter in what circumstances we may find ourselves, we can remain calm, peaceful and happy, knowing that Father is in *absolute* control. *This* is godly living. *This* is honest living – living in the truth that Father is completely in charge of all things. This *"godliness and honesty"* alone allows us to *"lead a quiet and peaceable life."*

> *That we may lead a quiet and peaceable life in all godliness and honesty* (I Timothy 2:2).

Our disposition towards *"all things"* and *"all men"* reflects our disposition toward God. A divinely aligned disposition will bring a change of quietness and peace to our life.

Many believers live in the turmoil created by the misjudging of the true source of *"all things."* Government, politics and economics are no exception. The political pundits agitate their spirits – displacing them from their God-given *"quiet and peaceable life."* Do not give way to such a snare!

Don't let them agitate your spirit!

We know too much about things in this world to lean much on man. ... Every single item of history today is certainly in accord with God's intention, even though it seems that almost all of it is contrary to His will. Only if that is true can we have universal reconciliation. God can save all mankind eventually only if He keeps the reins in His hand. All will not simply be saved, but reconciled, glorifying God. All this is fulfilling God's intention. ... So let us give thanks for it, no matter how bad it seems to be. When we realize this, then we can live in this insane asylum, and we will not quarrel with the inmates. ... We acknowledge that all is out of Him, as well as through Him and, consequently will be for Him in the great consummation.

A.E. Knoch (1874-1965)
Unsearchable Riches
Volume 38, 1947

Chapter 17

Giving Thanks for President Obama

I exhort therefore, that ... giving of thanks, be made for all men; for kings, and for all who are in authority (I Timothy 2:1-2).

God is at the center of all human activity – including human governments – for,

HE is a great King over all the earth (Psalm 47:2).

Therefore, whoever has power is whom He has placed in power, for He

Rules in the kingdom of men, and gives it to whomsoever He will (Daniel 4:17, 25).

There is no power but of God: the powers that be are ordained of God (Romans 13:1).

Not only is whom He has chosen in power, but He directs their very heart as well, for,

The king's heart is in the hand of the Lord, as the rivers of water: He turns it wherever He will (Proverbs 21:1).

Therefore, for example, in the United States – as I write these words – Barack Hussein Obama II is God's chosen vessel at this time. He is God's instrument, and our divinely ordained attitude towards him, as with George Bush and Bill Clinton before him, is to pray and give thanks for him:

I exhort therefore, that, first of all, supplications, prayers, intercessions and giving of thanks be made for all men; for kings, and for all who are in authority; that we may lead a quiet and peaceable life in all godliness and honesty (I Timothy 2:1-2).

Interestingly enough, Paul wrote these words in the context of one of the most evil, corrupt, brutal rulers who ever lived.

Concerning the Roman Emperor Nero, James Stalker wrote,

He was a man who, in a bad world, had attained the eminence of being the very worst and meanest being in it – a man stained with every crime, the murder of his own mother, of his wives and of his best benefactors. — *The Life of St. Paul*, pages 142-143

H.I. Hester, in his work *The Heart of the New Testament* (1964), elaborates,

Rome had several tyrannical and corrupt emperors but Nero was the worst. He was immoral, vicious, selfish and despotically cruel. He came to the throne in A.D. 54 and ruled for fourteen years ... He will go down in history as one of the most despicable men ever to rule over a people
...

Historians are generally agreed that it was Nero who burned the city of Rome. He labored under the delusion that he was a genius in music and that his compositions would become immortal if only he had sufficient inspiration. Feeling that a great conflagration would provide the inspiration he had the city set on fire. It is said that he sat on an elevated porch overlooking the city and attempted to play the violin as he watched the city burn. This fire broke out on July 19th in the year 64 and raged for six days. Much to the surprise of Nero there was a violent reaction among the people and he hastened to attach the blame for this on the Christians. Immediately thereafter serious persecution broke out against these Christian people. It took real courage to be a Christian now as they were granted no protection by the law. These Neronian persecutions were unspeakably horrible. Christian men and women were burned, were cast to wild beasts in the amphitheater to entertain the populace. "'Nero lent his gardens for the purpose of exhibiting the tortures of the wretched victims, and at night he illuminated his grounds by the flames of burning Christians' – Foakes-Jackson, *Rise of Gentile Christianity*, page 50." (page 330)

This was the context of Paul's remarkable admonition to Timothy:

I exhort therefore, that, first of all, supplications, prayers, intercessions, and giving of thanks, be made for all men; for kings, and for all that are in authority; that we may lead a quiet and peaceable life in all godliness and honesty (I Timothy 2:1-2).

Paul was exhorting that the saints give thanks for Nero! Absolutely amazing! Yet, when we think about it, why wouldn't this be what Paul encouraged them to do, for did not Paul instruct them to give *"thanks always **for all things"*** (Ephesians 5:20)? Would this not have included Nero?

Paul clearly presents for us a spiritual attitude of thanksgiving: not just for "good" things, but for *all things* – and not just *IN* all things, but *FOR* all things. When we understand the great truth that *"all things are of God"* (II Corinthians 5:18), this is easy. When we embrace the fact that *"of Him, and through Him, and to Him, are all things"* (Romans 11:36), then we have no option but to thank Him *"for all things."*

Thanking God for *"all things,"* surely includes *"all men."* This is what Paul told Timothy, that the *"giving of thanks* [should] *be made for all men."* Then, Paul is specific not to exclude, but to include *"kings, and all who are in authority."* What does Paul then say that the results of such a disposition of thanksgiving would be?

> *That we may lead a quiet and peaceable life in all godliness and honesty.*

Paul here is not speaking of civil or social peace. The issue here is not that there would be national peace, but that *our hearts* would be aligned with God and His purpose, thus bringing quietness and peace to our hearts, and to the disposition of our lives.

No matter what national system in which we find ourselves, we can remain calm, peaceful and happy, knowing that Father is in absolute control. *THIS* is godly living. *THIS* is honest living – living in the truth that Father is completely in charge of all things. THIS *"godliness and honesty"* alone allows us to *"lead a quiet and peaceable life."*

Many believers live in the turmoil created by the misjudging of the true source of *"all things."* Government and politics are no exception. The political pundits agitate their spirits – displacing them from their God-given *"quiet and peaceable life."* Do not give way to such a snare!

ALL MEN

Listen to some of what Paul taught concerning *"all men."*

* We Are to Love *"All Men"*

  The Lord make you to increase and abound in love one toward another, and toward **all men,** *even as we do toward you* (I Thessalonians 3:12).

* We Are to Be Gentle to *"All Men"*

  The servant of the Lord must not strive; but be gentle to **all men** (II Timothy 2:24).

* We Are to Show Meekness to *"All Men"*

  To speak evil of no man, to be no brawlers, but gentle, showing all meekness to **all men** (Titus 3:2).

* We are to Give Thanks for *"All Men"*

  I exhort therefore, that … giving of thanks, be made for all men (I Timothy 2:1).

Our disposition towards all men really reflects our disposition toward God. Paul could give thanks for Nero. Why not start by giving thanks for Obama today? If it is heartfelt, it will bring a change of quietness and peace to your life.

That's what the verses say.

We are exhorted to walk worthy of the calling wherewith we have been called (Ephesians 4:1). This implies the **knowledge** of our **"calling."** It is a **"high calling."** The word rendered **"high"** is the same as that rendered **"above"** in Colossians 3:2, **"Set your affection on things above, not on things on the earth."** We are called of God from beneath to above, from earth to heaven.

We are not as those that dwell on the earth. Moralists, philanthropists and politicians all recognize something valuable in Christianity, and use it as helpful to their own ends; and thus has Christianity been dragged down from its lofty eminence, until almost all that is distinctive is lost amidst as many elements which are foreign.

William Kelly (1820-1906)
Sin of Sectarianism

Chapter 18

Living as God's Sons

Do all things without murmurings and disputings: that you may be blameless and harmless, the sons of God, without rebuke, in the midst of a crooked and perverse nation, among whom you shine as lights in the world; Holding forth the Word of Life; that I may rejoice in the day of Christ, that I have not run in vain, neither labored in vain (Philippians 2:14-16).

L et us notice some of the particulars of this passage.

- We are identified here as *"the sons of God."*

  This is our approach to life. This is who we are. This is our God-given reality. This is where we live.

- We are the sons of God "*in the midst of a crooked and perverse nation.*"

The details of life will not be easy because we are in hostile surrounds. We are the sons of the Exiled King.

- We are "*among*" them to "*shine as lights in the world.*"

> Everything will be okay in the end. If it's not okay, then it's not the end.

We are not seen by those around us for who we really are. We stand shoulder-to-shoulder, side-by-side "*among*" them. As sons, we are providing the light for this dark domain. The light is not so that we may illuminate ourselves; it is that we may illuminate our way to walk, thus providing illumination on the Savior for those "*among*" whom we live.

- We are "*holding forth the Word of Life.*"

The way that we enlighten our path and those "*around*" us is by holding forth "*the Word of Life.*" We hold the Word in front of us. As David wrote, "*Your Word is a **lamp** to my feet, and a **light** to my path*" (Psalm 119:105). As we keep the truth of God's Word ever before our eyes, throughout the course of our day, we are able to *see* how to walk as sons.

- We will be able to "*rejoice in the day of Christ.*"

The culmination of our daily walking in the light of our Father will not be fully realized until "*the day of Christ.*" Then we will be able to rejoice fully in our sojourn here.

- Our lives will not have been *"run in vain."*

  What will be the reason for our *"rejoicing in the day of Christ"*? That our race and labor was not in vain! We are saved from the vanity of the sons of Adam – living daily in our sonship position in Christ.

Now, having looked through this passage briefly, we will return to the first phrase. We deliberately passed over it, because we believe that in it lies the very key to the passage. Look at how it begins:

Do all things without murmurings and disputings:
THAT *you may be ...*

All that Paul says afterward is preceded by what it is that we actually *"do."* We are instructed by Paul to *"do all things without murmurings and disputings."* This is the attitude and approach that we are to have regarding the circumstances of life, as sons of the Father.

Here is what we must ever keep *"holding forth"* before our eyes: we *are* the sons of God. Those around us are unaware of this astonishing fact. We did not have a royal motorcade escorting us to our workplace this morning. Those who were in the elevator with us this afternoon were unaware that we co-own the universe. We were not ushered to the front of the checkout line this evening at the grocery store. Our neighbors know nothing of our true identity. Even if we tell them, they would not understand. It is hidden from their eyes.

> Occupy the position that God gave you.

Those who are irritated and confused, troubled and depressed from the vanity of being a descendant of Adam will be short with us. In their frustration of the endless cycle of vanity they often will be hurtful, mean and vindictive. None of this is true of who we are. We have a life full of meaning and purpose, joy and peace, because we are a descendant of the one true and living God.

> Let us not confuse the process with the end.
>
> — A.E. Knoch

We are the people of hope on the planet. We have, as our birthright as the sons of God, the blessed fruit of His Spirit: love, joy, peace, longsuffering, gentleness, goodness, faith, meekness and temperance. Yet when we join the descendants of Adam in their misery-ways, we deny all that God has made us – the real us. We need to remember to walk through this dark world as the *"children of light."*

> *You were sometimes darkness, but now are you light in the Lord:* **walk as children of light:** *for the fruit of the Spirit is in all goodness and righteousness and truth* (Ephesians 5:8-9).

> *You are all* **the children of light,** *and* **the children of the day:** *we are not of the night, nor of darkness* (I Thessalonians 5:5).

We do not walk in the darkness. We walk in the light of all that we have and are in Christ! To murmur and dispute is, in all reality, not to believe these truths. Walking in this light of who we are is what it means to walk in His Spirit – just to allow Him to live His life (who we really are) in us. After teaching us the fruit of the Spirit, Paul says:

> *If we live in the Spirit, let us also walk in the Spirit* (Galatians 5:25).

Living the fruit of His Spirit is walking in the Spirit. It is not an *effort* – *trying* to work up this fruit in our lives. Instead it is *fruit* – the byproduct of *His life* flowing through us. It is His product.

AWAITING OUR UNVEILING

The earnest expectation of the creature waits for the manifestation of the sons of God (Romans 8:19).

Let us notice some of the particulars of this passage.

- We are not yet manifest as the sons of God.

  The world does not know who we are. Our sonship is completely hidden from them at this time.

- One day we shall be made manifest.

  In the resurrection God will reveal to all of creation who His sons are. This will be a glorious coronation day.

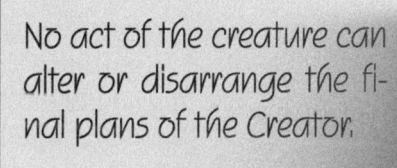

No act of the creature can alter or disarrange the final plans of the Creator.

— Arthur P. Adams

- The rest of creation is awaiting this manifestation.

  The whole creation groans and is eagerly awaiting redemption. They do not know about, nor understand this deliverance, but it is to be found in our manifestation. What a glorious day this fulfillment will be for *all* of creation.

Until our manifestation is made, the rest of God's creation does not know who we are. As we walk through the circumstances of our days, they will *not* reflect our true identity. In fact, we shall not be exempt from all of the apparent vanities of this *dark*land. We shall have our share of the *dark*side – suffering, pain, discouragement, difficulties, weariness, pressure and the like – but we are not defined by their details; and although we are beckoned to the contrary on every side, we have a higher life – the high-life from above, from the *light*land. We are called to walk in this radiant light.

As we go through the various details of this earthly life, let us not forget who we really are. Let us remember our divine calling and position as God's Own sons. Let that be our day-by-day, moment-by-moment focus; and let us hold forth the Word of life, so that we can see clearly who we are, and how we are to walk as honorable sons of God.

Ours is *"the high calling of God in Christ Jesus"* (Philippians 3:14).

Chapter 19

Postscript

*T*his is a note to those who may find themselves in harmony with some of the material presented in this work. We have no corner on truth, nor does anyone else. None possess all truth infallibly. Therefore we should seek to fellowship with all who love the Lord Jesus Christ and take pleasure in His precious Word.

I truly love all that love the glorious Emmanuel, and though I cannot depart from those principles which I believe are clearly revealed in the Book of God, yet I can cheerfully associate with those that differ from me, if I have reason to think that they are united to our common Head. — George Whitefield

We must remember that knowledge puffs up, but love builds up.[1] Let us dare not use anything that we may learn and hold dear as a tool of division between us and other believers. May we always remember that contentious *debate* has its place – it

---

1. I Corinthains 8:1.

belongs to the realm of the *flesh*.[2] We should never use these issues *against* a fellow member of *Christ's* Body. God the Father has *received* all of those who are *in Christ*.[3] Can we do any less?

> *Wherefore receive each other, as Christ also received us to the glory of God* (Romans 15:7).

---

2. *cf.* Romans 1:29; II Corinthians 12:20.
3. Romans 14:3.

Appendix 1

Heaping Coals of Fire

Recompense to no man evil for evil. Provide things honest in the sight of all men. If it be possible, as much as lies in you, live peaceably with all men. Dearly beloved, avenge not yourselves, but rather give place to wrath: for it is written, "Vengeance is Mine; I will repay, says the Lord." Therefore if your enemy hungers, feed him; if he thirsts, give him drink: for in so doing you will heap coals of fire on his head. Be not overcome of evil, but overcome evil with good (Romans 12:17-21).

IT IS SO AMAZING how man's negative view of God flavors the reading of the Scriptures. It leads to the assumption that the phrase *"heap coals of fire on his head"* is to be viewed in a negative light. Religion is so misleading.

Rome used such passages as this to carry out their Inquisitions and burnings at the stake. Many Protestant commentators have promoted their own negative view as well:

Coals of fire are doubtless emblematical of pain ... Burning coals heaped on a man's head would be expressive of intense agony. So the apostle says that the effect of doing good to an enemy would be to produce pain.

— Albert Barnes (1798-1870)
Barnes' Notes on the Bible

By coals of fire heaped upon the head, others understand a sin-punishing fire. "*Thou shalt heap coals of fire*," that is, the fire of divine vengeance, upon his head, by making his malice and hatred against thee more inexcusable.

— William Burkitt (1650-1703)
Burkitt's Expository Notes

Bring down the greater vengeance from God upon him.

— Matthew Poole (1624-1679)
Poole's Commentary on the Holy Bible

This passage is a perfect example of how the Father alerts us to the error in our thinking. So, what *is* wrong with this picture?

We really need to ask ourselves, what does this passage mean in light of all that we know about the Father – of His ultimate victory in bringing all things into harmony with Himself, and using us as His vessels of mercy?

May I ask a simple question here? What would be the natural purpose of "*coals of fire*"? For instance, if I was to have "*coals of fire*" in my own home, would I do so for a *negative* purpose, or for a *positive* one? Would my purpose be for punishment? For shame? For destruction? To produce guilt? To produce pain? No, of course not. A wise man would use "*coals of fire*" in his home for none of these reasons. He would use them to warm his home. Why should we think any differently about its use here? Isn't our life of goodness and kindness designed by the Father to "warm up" those with whom we share His life? He uses us as instruments of kindness to warm the coldness, and melt the hardness of their hearts.

The Methodist commentator Adam Clarke (1760-1832), wrote fittingly regarding this passage,

> *"Thou shalt heap coals of fire upon his head"* – not to consume, but to melt him into kindness; a metaphor taken from smelting metallic ores.

Here is what another has written regarding the true nature of this passage:

> An enemy in distress, instead of calling for hate and vengeance, is a special opportunity for the display of God's grace. The *"morsel,"* a special portion of food with which a host favored an honored guest, was a token of esteem and consideration. Mercy might provide an enemy with food, but grace accompanies the gift with every mark of love and honor. This is the way in which God vanquished our enmity, hence we should do likewise.
>
> — A.F. Knoch (1874-1965)
> *Concordant Commentary*

Speaking to the broader theme of the passage, others have written:

> He tells us to pour coals of fire on our enemies' heads. Those coals of fire are love! (Romans 12:20).
>
> — Gary Amirault
> *Tentmakers*

Does this rob God of anything? Not even of revenge, for if bread to the hungry be the divine method of heaping coals of fire, so does God Himself revenge Himself upon His enemies by *loving* them!

— Alan Burns (1884-1929)
  Is It of God?

A FIGURE OF SPEECH

Now what about the actual phrase *"heap coals of fire on his head."* What does this actually mean? We are told that this is a Jewish figure of speech that has, for the most part, been lost to the western mind:

Paul says that if we give food and drink to our enemies, we shall be heaping *"coals of fire on their heads."* To us this doesn't sound like forgiveness, but like taking "vengeance." In the Bible lands almost everything is carried on the head – water jars, baskets of fruit, vegetables, fish or any other article. Those carrying the burden rarely touch it with the hands, and they walk through crowded streets and lanes with perfect ease. In many homes the only fire they have is kept in a *brazier* which they use for simple cooking as well as for warmth. They plan to always keep it burning. If it should go out, some member of the family will take the brazier to a neighbor's house to borrow fire. Then she will lift the brazier to her head and start for home. If her neighbor is a generous woman, she will heap the brazier full of coals. To feed an enemy and give him drink was like heaping the empty brazier with live coals – which meant food, warmth and almost life itself to the person or home needing it, and was the symbol of finest generosity.

— B.M. Bowen
  Strange Scriptures that Perplex the Western Mind

We, Westerners, usually picture vengeance when we think of pouring hot coals on someone's heads. The Semites pictured something completely different. We, Westerners, must break some of our traditions, if we are to ever come to a deep understanding of the God of the Bible. It is full of beautiful pictures like this one.

— Gary Amirault
Tentmakers

The phrase *"heap coals of fire on his head"* is a part of the quote from Proverbs 25:21-22. Farrar Fenton's (1903) translation of the passage in Proverbs takes the phrase *"heap coals of fire on his head"* in its literal meaning, thus explaining the Jewish figure of speech, rather than translating it:

And a fire besides for his needs.

Although popular translations of this entire passage may often lead readers to a "punishment" view toward mankind,[1] we have actually been instructed *not* to recompense *"evil for evil"* (Romans 12:17), but to *"overcome evil with good"* (Romans 12:21). This is the divine plan of the ages – **"overcome evil with good"** – for, *"love never fails!"* (I Corinthians 13:8).

Jesus instructed His disciples to love their enemies and be a blessing to them:

But I say to you, Love your enemies, bless them who curse you, do good to them who hate you, and pray for

---

1. Romans 12:17-21 from the *Bible Student's Version*:
   Return to no one evil for evil. Display nobility before all men. If possible, as much as lies in you, cultivate peace with all mankind. Dearly beloved, don't retaliate, but recede from the place of anger: for it is written, "Vindication belongs to Me; I will make it up to you," says the Lord. Therefore if your enemy hungers, feed him; if he thirsts, give him drink: for in so doing you will heap coals of fire on his head. Don't be conquered by evil, but conquer evil with good.

them who despitefully use you, and persecute you (Matthew 5:44).

On what basis did He do so? Because this is the very nature of the Father!

Be therefore perfect, even as your Father which is in heaven is perfect (Matthew 5:48).

"*God is love*" (I John 4:8, 16), and His love has been "*shed abroad in our hearts*" (Romans 5:5), that we may "*walk in love*" (Ephesians 5:2), so that as the Father's "*vessels of mercy*" (Romans 9:23) we would be a "*blessing*" to those around us:

Love your enemies, bless them who curse you, do good to them who hate you (Matthew 5:44).

Bless them who persecute you: bless, and curse not (Romans 12:14).

Being reviled, we bless (I Corinthians 4:12).

See that none render evil for evil to any man; but ever follow that which is good, both among yourselves, and to all men (I Thessalonians 5:15).

Not rendering evil for evil, or railing for railing: but contrariwise blessing (I Peter 3:9).

This is our "*high calling of God in Christ Jesus*" (Philippians 3:14)!

Appendix 2

John Calvin's Geneva

by – Gene Edwards

GENEVA WAS *RULED* with an iron fist by twenty men. They were referred to as the Consistory Committee. (Yep, everybody was supposed to live *consistent* with how they were told to live.) Five of these men were pastors. Fifteen were church elders. Those twenty men ruled Geneva. Calvin ruled the twenty.

It was one of the most despotic governments in the history of the Western world. It was a police state. *All* the lives of all the people were under rule, scrutiny and surveillance. Invasion of privacy was the order of the day.

It seems that ministers believed our call is to make people sin as little as possible. Here is a man who lived by this idea. A city was forced to live that way, too.

A few rules? (People with weak hearts should not read beyond this point.)

Adultery: Death by burning at the stake.

Witchcraft: Ditto

Missing Church Services Frequently: Death by being burned alive.

Heresy: Death by being burned alive.

Heresy defined: *Anyone who dared disagree with Calvin's Theology.*

(I think we are seeing a pattern develop here.)

Everybody got off the first time. Nobody got off the third time.

Anyone could be brought before the Consistory. Suspicions were tantamount to guilt. You could be imprisoned at will.

You were told what kind of clothes to wear. Dress was by *caste* (that is, by your standing in society).

Children had to be named after Bible characters. A gentleman refused and named his child something else – he went to jail for four days.

No rouge or "powdering," no jewelry, no immodest dress. (Guess who decided what was and wasn't!) No cards, lace, hunting. No books that were not religious. No dancing. No singing of non-Christian songs.

If a child struck his parents, he was beheaded. But, as always, sex was a big no-no. Any sex outside of marriage and you were drowned. Pregnant outside of wedlock, the same. The man was drowned too. You don't believe? Calvin's stepson was caught and drowned. His daughter-in-law was caught and drowned; so were the other two people involved.

Tenderhearted soul, this Calvin.

Fourteen women accused of witchcraft were burned alive.

Reasoning behind such cruel punishment? I quote Calvin:

> When the Catholics are so harsh and violent in their defense of their *superstitions,* are not Christ's magistrates shamed to do less in defense of the truth?

I think Jesus would have been burned alive in Geneva.

Excerpts taken from Gene Edward's *How to Meet,* chapter 24.

Appendix 3

Jury Ducy

NOT LONG AFTER finishing my first series of articles on government in the Bible Student's Notebook (issues #38 - #44) in 1999, I received a letter and questionnaire regarding jury duty from the local Jury Commissioners.

I thought that a copy of my letter of response might be of some help and encouragement to those who find themselves in harmony with our conclusions.

Clyde L. Pilkington, Jr.
111 Charity Lane
Gladstone VA 24553

November 22, 2000
Jury Commissioners
Amherst County
PO Box 462
Amherst, VA 24521

Dear Honorable Sirs:

I feel that a letter of explanation is in order to accompany the attached questionnaire. First, I would like to explain the reason for my delay in responding.

The address that you have is my former one. We have moved to the corrected address on the questionnaire.

Second, I would like to explain the dilemma that I find myself in.

Upon moving to Amherst County in 1996 I registered to vote. But as you may be able to tell from voting records, I never have exercised that function. This is due to personal convictions that have developed. I have come to believe that I, as a citizen of heaven (Philippians 3:20), have a conflict of interest when it comes to voting and other "decision" making processes that relate to government.

Let me be clear that I am not opposed in any fashion to human government. I believe that human government is ordained of God and that you and other government servants are indeed *"ministers of God"* (Romans 13:4), and that you have the full right to bear the *"sword in vain."* So, the conflict that I have does not come from the rightful role of government.

Instead, my conflict comes from my own role as a member of Christ's Body (I Corinthians 12:13) and an ambassador of Jesus Christ (II Corinthians 5:20). I find that the principles that guide me as a member of Christ's Body place me in direct conflict with the principles (equally divinely appointed) of human government. God has called me to *"recompense no man evil for evil"* (Romans 12:17), and thus to a ministry of *"grace"* (Ephesians 3:2), and *"forgiveness"* (Ephesians 4:32).

I suppose one of the best ways to explain this conflict to you is by means of the commonly used phrase, "the separation of church and state." I have come to see and understand that as a believer in the Lord Jesus Christ I am the church. Paul, the apostle, defines the church as the Body of Christ (Ephesians 1:22-23).

As a member of His Body I am – along with all other believers – the church. I believe that there is a clear line of separation between church and state. I believe that I have a distinct role to fulfill, as does the state. Therefore, since I believe that my role *"in Christ's stead"* (II Corinthians 5:20) is one of *"grace"* and *"forgiveness,"* I believe that I have strong conflicts of interest that would disqualify me from serving as a juror.

I do not mean to imply that I would not serve. In fact, I would find no difficulty in simple decisions of right and wrong (I Corinthians 6:2); but there would be clear conflicts of interest as to the response of *"grace"* and *"forgiveness."*

Since coming to this understanding, I have written extensively concerning the role of a believer in Christ in relationship to human government. These writings have been published in a periodical called the *Bible Student's Notebook* (a publication that has been in circulation for twelve years). I would be glad to submit the past issues that cover this topic if they would be of any further help in this process.

I look forward to hearing from you on this matter.

Thank you for your kind consideration.

Reminded of my privilege of keeping you in my prayers (I Timothy 2:1-2).

I am sincerely yours,

Clyde L Pilkington, Jr.

_____

I never received a response from the Jury Commissioners to my letter, neither was I ever summoned for jury duty.

I also used the same letter since living in PA. As with the jury authorities in VA, I never received a response, nor have been summoned for duty.

Appendix 4

The Story of the Paulicians

A Lesson from History

THE PAULICIANS WERE believers who lived outside of the religious system. They were called "Paulicians" by their adversaries due to their emphasis on Paul's epistles. They were one of the greatest preserved testimonies of faithfulness in church history, even though it was their enemies who preserved their account. Theirs was a testimony that spanned six centuries.

I first began searching for the record of their testimony more than 25 years ago. I have been able to find only bits and pieces along the way, but it is an amazing patchwork. Their enemies told many lies about them, and accused them of many things. When the dust settles from all of the historical rhetoric, we can see a composite picture of saints who followed Paul as their apostle, lived as the church (rather than "going to church"), rejected religious tradition and ordinances, and believed in the ultimate salvation of all.

What follows here is a collection of quotations that bring these saints into some historical light.

All through the ages God has had His people, who cherished His truth and witnessed for Him. Known by different names at different times and in different places: scattered abroad singly, in small companies, or in communities, they kept the faith.

One of the most noted examples of those who struggled against the advancing heathen darkness as it gradually overspread the Church is found in the people known as the "Paulicians."

By whatever name we may be called or known, we are, in witnessing for the teaching of God in the Pauline Epistles, the true successors of the ancient Paulicians: holding aloft the banner; holding forth the same Word; and holding fast the same truth.

— E.W. Bullinger (1837-1913)
  The Paulicians: A Lesson From the Past
  Things to Come, October, 1901

-o-0-o-

Whatever opinions may be held about the Paulicians, it is generally conceded that they had a particular respect for the authority of the Bible, for the apostle Paul and his writings, were a devout and earnest people, and bore a strong witness against the unsavory practices of the Catholic Church. Their enemies testified against them, but their lives testified of Christ.

In assessing the character of the Paulicians historians have tended too readily to accept uncritically what has been said and written against them by their enemies. The history of the Roman Church in its dealings with those who refused to bow to its dominion is a sordid tale of pillage and persecution. Not only did it seek to destroy those who opposed it, but also to bring the very memory of their names into ignominy by the most gross accusations, and to obliterate what they themselves wrote or anything written about them in their favor. It is hardly surprising, therefore, that much more literature survives which condemns than commends them.

The great struggle of later centuries to produce the Scriptures in the languages of the ordinary people illustrates most aptly the methods which Rome employed to maintain her authority over the souls of men. Copies of the Scripture were hunted out and consigned to the flames, and along with them those who were responsible for their publication and dissemination, if they refused to recant from the "sin" of having sought to spread the Word of God. These same methods were generously employed in the days of the Paulicians.

The Paulicians accepted no central authority, they looked to God as their Head, and they were built up and strengthened spiritually by teachers who moved from place to place to minister in a manner similar to Paul. They did not draw up any code of doctrine to which they had commonly to subscribe as a basis of unity. Their spiritual unity lay in the life which they had in Christ, a life which manifested itself in their daily walk and witness. They owned a professed respect for the Word of God, which they accepted as their guide.

— John W. Kennedy
   Torch of the Testimony
   1983, pp. 109-110

-o-0-o-

There were believers who stood out strongly against the idolatry, sacramentalism, and other prevailing errors of the Catholic Church. They appear on the historical scene in the middle of the seventh century as "Paulicians" in the region of Mesopotamia. Why they were named "Paulicians" is not exactly known, but it may simply have been because of their respect for the apostle Paul and his writings. The Catholic Church ascribed to them all sorts of erroneous doctrines, if we can believe those whose lives denied the truths they professed. Most of what has reached us has come down from their critics.

— Kenneth Latourette
   A History of Christianity
   1975, p. 318

-o-0-o-

[To the Paulicians] baptism means only the baptism of the Spirit; the communion with the body and blood of Christ is only a communion with His Word and doctrine.

— Philip Schaff
   History of the Christian Church
   1910, Vol. 4, p. 577

-o-0-o-

The Paulicians equally denied the name of "church" to buildings of wood or stone.

— *Encyclopedia Britannica*
   Paulicians
   1959

-o-0-o-

The [Paulicians] had no order of clergymen, nor had they councils, or any other institutions. Their teachers were all equals in rank; and were distinguished by no rights, or prerogatives, or insignia.

— John L. Von Mosheim
  Institutes of Ecclesiastical History, Ancient and Modern
  1869, Volume 2, p. 103

-o-0-o-

Paulicians, named probably from a high regard for the Apostle Paul, opposed the formalism of the Greek Church and the prelatic [cleric] system: rejected images, crosses, relics, fasts, monasticism, priesthood, outward observance of the two sacraments and saint worship; they were severely persecuted; many scattered through all Southern Europe, and received various new names.

— W.M. Blackburn
  History of the Christian Church
  1879, p. 332

-o-0-o-

[The Paulicians] rejected all outward means of grace, such as baptism and the Lord's Supper, and especially the later developments of sacramentarianism.

— John Moncrief
  A Short History of the Christian Church
  1908, p. 183

-o-0-o-

E.B. Elliott, author of the 19th century commentary on the Revelation [*Horæ Apocalypticæ*, (London: 1863)], gives a synopsis of Paulician history. Elliott traces the origin of the Paulicians through one Constantine [not to be confused with the Roman Emperor, Constantine the Great], in A.D. 654, not Paul of Samosata, the heretical Manichæn Bishop, as their enemies held. Rather, the Paulicians derived their name from the great teacher of election by grace, the Apostle Paul.

— Randy Winburn
History of the Paulician Iconoclast,[1] p. 18

-o-0-o-

It is generally agreed that the word Paulician is formed from the name of the great apostle of the Gentiles. They preached against images, relics and the rotten wood of the cross. They were not fit to live. The Catholics gained their object! An edict was issued under the regency of Theodora [A.D. 842], which decreed that the Paulicians should be exterminated by fire and sword. Her inquisitors explored the cities and mountains of the lesser Asia, and executed their commission in the most cruel manner. It is affirmed by both civil and ecclesiastical historians, that, in a short reign, one hundred thousand Paulicians were put to death.

— Andrew Miller
Short Papers on Church History
1874, pp. 253-256

-o-0-o-

---

1. Iconoclasts – "Somebody who challenges or overturns traditional beliefs, customs, and values" (Encarta Dictionary).

They came to be called Paulicians because of the emphasis they laid on the Pauline Epistles instead of the "Hebrew Christian" Epistles. After 325 A.D., they viewed the Roman Catholic church and the Greek Orthodox church as Satanic, and they refused to tolerate images of any kind. However, the most significant thing about them was their wholesale rejection of the educated scholars. The Paulicians rejected the Catholic priesthood, the Catholic sacraments, the worship of relics and crosses, and they thought the "one baptism" of Ephesians four was the Holy Spirit putting the believer into Christ: they were the Stamites and Bullingerites of their day. Under severe persecution they moved into Bulgaria and the Balkan mountains and from thence to north Italy and Yugoslavia to produce Christians called Waldenses and Albigenses. The Paulicians in Italy were called Paterini or Cathari; in France they were called Bulgarians, Publicans and Albigenses.

— Peter S. Ruckman
The History of the New Testament Church
1984, Volume I, pp. 61, 234-235

-o-0-o-

Constantine's Edict Against the Paulicians:

Understand now, by this present statute, you Novatians, Valentinians, Marcionites, Paulicians, and Montanists, and all the rest of you who devise and support heresies by means of your private assemblies ... that your offenses are so hateful and altogether atrocious that a single day would be insufficient to tolerate your deadly errors, we hereby give you warning that none of you are to meet together hereafter. We have therefore ordered that your meeting places be taken from you. And you are expressly forbidden to hold your superstitions and senseless meetings, not only in public, but also in private homes, or any other place.

— Eusebius' *Constantine,*
Book 3, chapters 64, 65

-o-0-o-

The doctrines, character and history of the Paulicians have been subjects of great controversy; but they have not been allowed to speak for themselves to posterity. Their writings were carefully destroyed by the Catholics, and they are known to us only through the reports of bitter enemies who brand them as heretics.

[The Paulicians were] greatly interested by the Pauline Epistles and resolved to secure a restoration of Christianity to its primitive Pauline form.

— A.H. Newman
A Manual of Church History
1899, pp. 379, 384

-o-0-o-

Not less than one hundred thousand of them [Paulicians] were put to death in Grecian Armenia. Of the tenets of this sect we have no knowledge except from their enemies.

— George Fisher
History of the Christian Church
1887, p. 162

-o-0-o-

Paul had spent his strength in planting and watching over the churches in Asia Minor. His toil was neither fruitless nor forgotten. Paul-like men, who were hailed as such by their contemporaries, and named *Paulikoi*, were stirred amid the growing need to imitate the Apostle to the Gentiles in his zeal and self-sacrifice for threatened truth and endangered souls.

They wrote out and multiplied copies of the Scriptures, especially of the Pauline Epistles. They spoke to loiterers in the market place, to travelers by the way, to all men wherever and whenever they had the opportunity. The people listened, were converted, and swept back the invading darkness. The movement swept over the cities and over the provinces, and alarmed the ecclesiastics and the statesmen even of distant Constantinople.

It speedily received a name. The followers of these *Paulikoi* were called *Paulikianoi,* and the Paulicians have taken their place in history, written by their ecclesiastical enemies and traducers [slanderers]. Armies were sent against them; and where the arguments of a heathenised Christianity were powerless to convince, the sword tried to terrify.

But the fleshly arm could not stay the truth. The harassed believers were refreshed by tokens that God was with them. One general, for instance, who knew nothing of the people or their beliefs till he was charged by the Emperors with their suppression, found, when he returned to Constantinople, that he had no rest till he laid down his appointment, forsook everything, and joined the people whom he had been sent to persecute.

They were banished from Asia Minor, and leaving their fatherland forever, passed over into Europe. They traveled along valleys and rivers of their new world, and settled in quietness here and there, taking with them, as their choicest treasure, the Word of God and the simplicity of worship for which their fathers died. The historian meets them again in communities and peoples that lived apart, and which Rome stamps out one by one. But the truth they preserved lived on, and burst forth at last in the splendor of the Reformation.

— John Urquhart
The Inspiration and Accuracy of the Holy Scriptures
1895, Book II, Chapter 1, pp. 101-103

-o-0-o-

Possibly a primitive form of Christianity cut off from later developments by geographic location, they are first heard of early in the second half of the seventh century on the eastern borders of the Empire, south of Armenia. They called themselves simply Christians and the designation Paulicians was given them by their enemies.

The Paulicians rejected the honors paid by Catholics to the Virgin Mary, the invocation of saints, icons, incense, candles and all material symbols. Most of that which has reached us [concerning them] has come down from their critics.

— K.S. Latourette
A History of Christianity
1953, pp. 299, 318

-o-0-o-

They [the Paulicians] abhorred the use of images, of relics, pompous ceremonies, and ecclesiastical domination;

and they dispensed with even the rites of water baptism and the Lord's supper. Their preachers were distinguished by no title from their brethren; and no superiority was allowed.

Their total disrespect of images and relics, their contempt of all those artifices by which the craft got their living, kindled against them the most implacable hatred; and the orthodox emperors of the East resolved on their complete extermination.

They sustained a bloody persecution, with a patience and inoffensive meekness that converted some even of their executioners. But all human endurance may at length be overcome; and when that sanguinary zealot, the empress Theodora, succeeded to the regency of the East, during her son's minority, she drove them beyond the bounds of forbearance. In those parts of Asia Minor where they abounded, and in Armenia, she confiscated their goods, and put to death by the sword, the gibbet and the flames, more than a hundred thousand of their number, making them expire slowly by a variety of the most excruciating torments.

Towards the close of the century, the power of the Paulicians was effectually broken, and they were obliged to seek security in the fastnesses of the Armenian mountains. But they had already obtained a permanent footing in Europe under the name of Albanenses, Albigenses, Cathari, and, perhaps, Waldenses. This mongrel race, it is well known, spread through Italy, France and Germany; and for a long period suffered from the Church all the cruelty that cunning could devise and power inflict.

[The Paulicians] disclaim[ed] all tyranny over the consciences of men. [The Paulicians] rejected the Jewish [books], as they called the Old Testament; but the New Testament, which in the orthodox church had almost disappeared from the laity, they received as the inestimable and only volume of sacred Scripture, and enjoined its diligent perusal on all the people. It is probable; however, that they "disowned" the two Epistles of St. Peter, and the Revelation of St. John; and it is certain that their favorite books were the writings of St. Paul: from whom they, perhaps, took their name of Paulicians.

It is probable that many of them held, in some form, the doctrine of the salvation of all souls; for of this they are accused by the Catholic writers, who also assert that they denied a future judgment and future punishment.

— Hosea Ballou
  The Ancient History of Universalism
  1829, pp. 306-313

-o-0-o-

In France they [the Paulicians] were called Weavers, Poor of Lyons, Waldenses, and Albigenses; in Flanders, Piphles; and in Germany, Cathari. They were at Bonn, and in the diocese of Cologne; they abounded near the Alps and Pyrenees; they were greatly diffused through Provence and in Tholouse; they existed in Spain; and they spread through Lombardy to Padua and Florence, and some had even entered Naples.

— Sharon Turner
  The History of England
  1815, Volume II, pp. 381-382

-o-0-o-

One group which struggled against the gathering heathen darkness that was gathering was called the Paulicians by their contemporaries. They were very zealous and they copied Paul's writings and distributed them.

— Oscar Baker (1898-1987)
Truth for Today
1957, Volume 9, Number 6

-o-0-o-

WHATEVER HAPPENED TO THE PAULICIANS?

The Paulicians covered many countries of Europe and Asia Minor. They endured severe persecution with remarkable growth. We can trace many other groups of believers directly to their faithfulness. Yet whatever became of them? Where did they go? What happened to them?

After some 600 years, according to E.W. Bullinger, they lost their perspective as to their purpose and function on earth. He tells us that,

The Paulicians were unconquerable 'til, goaded by ages of injustice, they betook themselves to the sword. From that day their strength decayed until they were finally over-powered.[2]

2. E.W. Bullinger, The Paulicians: A Lesson From the Past, *Things To Come*, October, 1901.

Appendix 5

Politicians? or Paulicians?

by — Alan Burns (1884-1929)

THE TERM "PAULICIAN" may be misunderstood, especially if it be taken to represent an *"I am of Paul"* sectarianism. When even *"I am of Christ"* is frowned upon by the
great apostle as being sectarian and heretical, we may well
be assured that such a caste usage of it is nothing but a form
of wretched religious snobbery. However, we cannot find a
better term to distinguish the gold from the tinsel in modern
Christendom than by using this word to describe those who
have shared Paul's knowledge of the divine mysteries and adopted Paul's attitude toward the world movements.

"The gospel of the kingdom" has its *political* elements, for the
kingdom of which it treats is a real kingdom, with a real King,
a real capital, a real government, a real law, and is, in fact,
not only *as real* as but *more real* than the kingdom of Great
Britain today. Because of this, whatever fractional portion
of the kingdom gospel can be made to apply to the political
theories of the modern *social church* is taken and tortured
into seeming acquiescence with them. Yet, in order to do so,
a very vital ingredient of the kingdom gospel is kept out, *viz.,*
its eschatology. The ethics of the kingdom gospel, such ethics as may be found in the Sermon on the Mount, and rep-

resenting an intensification of the Mosaic law's demand for perfection, condemns rather than saves the man who will try to climb up to heaven on the ladder of the Beatitudes. What man needed was not a demand but a supply, and even a golden-runged ladder is of no avail to one crippled from birth. It may then be suggested that when the modern church takes the ethics and refuses the eschatology of *"the gospel of the kingdom"* it embraces the part that, of itself alone, condemns and repudiates the very portion, or ingredient, that contains the hope of salvation.

If the Law on the Mount through Moses was a *political* failure in bringing in *social* righteousness, because of the unspiritual state of the nation to which it was given, then surely the Law on the Mount through Christ would be a greater *political* failure if given to the Gentiles, which we know it was not.

Lot still is seated by Sodom's gate, and his sons of today have the *social gospel* of their ancient sire, for the time is not yet ripe for the taunt to be hurled, *"This one fellow came in to sojourn, and he will needs be a judge"* (Genesis 19:9). Lot had no gospel for the people of Sodom, nor did he possess any divine authority whatever to mingle with their *political* gatherings; but he apparently found an easy seat and an uneasy conscience when he associated with the city's elders at the gate. The "church" of today has, in its Bible, a gospel for the world, yet we find it in the role of a law-maker rather than a gospel preacher. Its preachers are trying to make citizens when they should be seeking to edify saints.

The saints of God are *aliens* here on earth. Let that sink in. No believer, as such, can be a Republican, for in his heart he believes in and is related to a kingdom. Republicanism is merely political Arminianism – it believes in human ability in some form. How can a rejected king became a member of a rebellious republic? If Christ be the King, forget not that we are His body. Individually we may be ambassadors entreating the world to be conciliated to God, but does England's ambassador to the United States vote? Can any ambassador legislate in the country to which he is sent? Of course not. Ambassadors come in to *"sojourn"* like Lot, and but few, if any, are guilty of making Lot's mistake.

How many of God's people have failed to see that, if you exercise a citizen's privileges in the time of peace, you must honorably fulfill a citizen's duties in the time of war! Ballots and bayonets are logically united: the ballot is the means whereby the majority makes law for the minority; and the bayonet is the weapon whereby the strong make law for the weak. You can no more preach the gospel with a ballot than you can with the point of a bayonet; but if, as a citizen, you claim the privilege of using the former, do not be surprised if your fellow-citizens expect you to face the duty of employing the latter.

Paul was no politician. Once, it is true, he claimed Roman citizenship, but see what happened thereafter. The events that followed after he claimed his "rights" quickly led to a conclusion of the preaching of the kingdom of God. If, as a Roman citizen, he received Roman protection for a season, it is also true that as a Roman citizen he was put into a Roman prison, and ultimately as a Roman citizen suffered from the stroke of a Roman sword.

Paul had no political program. The cross put an end to man in the flesh. It assessed the natural man and declared him bankrupt. Bankrupt politically, morally, spiritually, totally. Instead of being a citizen of the world, he became a corpse in it: *"I am crucified with Christ."* As far as the world is concerned, the church of God is a cemetery full of nothing but dead men, and men with their names on tombstones do not run for political nominations.

The religious world of today prates much and often of the glories of "democracy"; yet the believer's hope is centered not in democracy but in Theocracy, not in man-ocracy but God-ocracy. If the reader is a "Paulician," or has learned the truth of Paul's epistles, he will not claim to be either a Republican, a Democrat or a Socialist, for God's choice and not his, God's vote and not his ballot has made him a member of the Theocratic party by the grace of God. *"Demas hath forsaken me, having loved this present world"* (II Timothy 4:10) would correctly describe the modern religious political attitude toward Paul's theocratic teaching.

Whitewashing the world is – alas! – the occupation of a "church" which should have learned by now that what the world needs is to be washed white. The whitewash may be applied now with this brush and then with that; but the "church" which thus would gloss over, and patch up, and do a tinkerer's job with a world whose disease is in its nature, and whose evils spring from its constitution, has repudiated the cross of Christ, the Theocratic hope of the Scriptures, God's way of dealing with the world's sin, and has become merely a political club instead of a Paulician church.

— *Unsearchable Riches,* Volume 15, page 273 (1924)

Appendix 6

The True Basis of World Peace

by – A.E. Knoch (1874-1965)

THE WORLD IS RUSHING to one of the greatest crises of human history. On all sides people are trying to make a new world. All of these efforts, without exception, are doomed to failure. Don't imagine that I am a pessimist. I am the biggest optimist you ever saw. There *will* be peace after a while, and it will be permanent. In the meantime there is going to be a terrible storm. It is said that in the middle of a tornado it is calm. This is the place and privilege of all who know the mind of God. I can see things going to ruin, yet be thankful for it and enjoy it. Not because people are suffering, but because of the prospect in view, because all of the travail that men are going through is preparing them to enjoy the glorious time at the consummation.

Now, the trouble with those who are trying to make a better world is, first of all, that they do not know where they are. If we only knew where we are, we would not be so distressed about where we are going. Things today are exactly where God intends them to be. When we see this, we have a chance to have peace – not the peace that men are talking about, but a real peace – the peace of God Himself. If you know God's plan, you will be satisfied with what God is doing, because He is riding the storm. He is controlling all events. The future is safe and satisfactory, no matter what the present may be.

We want to find out where we are; then we will be in a position to view the future and enjoy its tragic unfolding before our eyes. This holds true for practically everything. For instance, today you will find there are all sorts of ideas about what the Bible teaches, and especially about its prophecies. Men have been prophesying, depending upon the Bible, as to who is Antichrist. These prophets fail, because they do not know what God is about at the present time. Most people forget that God is doing a number of different things in various times and eras. Generally we are concerned with His administrations and dispensations. The Pauline space is a small, very lonely place, but it is where we ought to be. Alas, how many saints of today still live in long past administrations, under law, or in the days of our Lord, or in the book of Acts! Many have never reveled in their own glorious grace in Paul's epistles! Even after some have heard this teaching over and over again, they still wander away into far poorer pastures.

The saints are not exempt from the fate of the nations to which they belong. I do not wonder about the way things are today. Why, that is just what is to be expected! I am not a politician. I have never voted. But I am going to be a politician in the future. When we go up to our destined place among the celestials, then we will reign with Christ.

I want a real peace. Peace without God is no peace. God has appointed a Man and He is the Prince of Peace, and until He comes, thank God, there can be no peace worthy of the name.

— The True Basis of Peace
Unserachable Riches
Volume 37 (abridged)

Appendix 7

Our Rights

"We're Losing Our Rights and Freedoms"[1]

Paul understood what it meant to follow Christ when he told Timothy,

Everyone who wants to live a godly life in Christ Jesus will be persecuted (II Timothy 3:12).

Yet many Christian leaders seem to be incredulous when our government does something they interpret as persecution. We need to be reminded that the vast majority of Christians throughout history have had to function under the shadow of hostile, even cruel governments. An argument can be made, in fact, that such is God's design. Under His sovereign hand, persecution has often been the very instrument that has strengthened His people and spawned the spread of the gospel.

---

1. This section, "We're Losing Our Rights and Freedoms," is from *Bible Students Notebook #223*, adapted from the writings of Jon Zens and Cliff Bjork, *God and Country: The Dangers of Contemporary Christian Americanism*.

Rather than to protest and complain, therefore, we should,

> ... *rejoice in our sufferings, because we know that suffering produces perseverance; perseverance, character; and character, hope* (Romans 5:3-4).

The battle-cry to fight for our "eroding" civil freedoms, therefore, is misguided. Our civil liberties can and may be taken from us, but our gospel liberty in Christ cannot be taken from us.

As Paul well knew, a believer chained in solitary confinement is still "free" in the Lord. He is free to pray for those who misuse him and to take the opportunity to bring glory to Jesus Christ by his godly demeanor in the face of abuse. He is free not to render evil for evil and to return blessing in the face of cursing. And he is free, as opportunity arises, to feed and care for his enemy (Romans 12:20).

We must avoid the error of equating any civil liberties we may enjoy or lose with the spiritual liberty we *always* possess in Christ.

In II Corinthians 3:17, he was not referring to civil liberties granted by "godly" governments, but rather to the truly inalienable spiritual liberties that are the inheritance of all in whom the Spirit of the Lord dwells.

My Rights

A common phrase I hear from Christians in relation to politics is it is "my right" to have security, or it is "my right" to have low cost health care, or it is "my right" to have lower taxes, or it is "my right" to have religious freedom, etc.

It is not our right at all!

As Christians, we have no rights. The apostle Paul uses different words as it relates to the so-called "freedom" of the Christian. In I Corinthians 4:1, Paul uses the Greek word *huperetes* to describe our calling. This word was used to describe a 2nd or 3rd level galley slave who had no rights. If you've ever seen the movie Ben Hur, you will understand that a lower level rower was treated as worthless and had absolutely no rights whatsoever. In Ephesians 3:7, Paul uses the word *diakonos* which means "a lowly table waiter." A waiter is at the beck and command of those whom he serves. In Romans 1:1, Paul calls himself a *doulos* of Jesus Christ. This was one who was in the total service of another. This same idea is spoken of in Exodus 21 when a servant had his ear pierced in order to forever bind him to his master. As Christians, we are totally at the command of our Master, the Lord Jesus Christ. The days of our having personal rights are gone forever.

When so-called "religious rights" are taken away from us, we are shocked to think that this could happen in America. Fueled by such radio programs as "Focus on the Family," we write our Congressman and Senators and cry that our rights have been violated. Dear Christian, we have no rights! Oh, you may say that we have rights as American citizens, but beloved, we must make a choice ... we cannot serve both God and America. Either we are strangers in this world or we are not. Either our citizenship is in heaven or it is here in America.

We are not Americans first, then Christians second. We are not even Christians first, and Americans second. We are Christians, *period!* The "red, white and blue" is not our home. America is not our provider, and we should not expect the government to grant us rights – that privilege belongs to God alone. If we are blessed, let us thank God. If we are in a period of tribulation, let us seek God and submit to the work He has brought our way. When disaster struck Job, he understood Who was the Source of all things. He responded by saying,

> *The Lord gave, and the Lord has taken away. Blessed be the name of the Lord* (Job 1:21).

— Ken Eckerty
God is Not a Republican

Your Part

Now that you have read this book, it's your turn.

If the truths presented here have helped you, don't let these truths die in your hands.

Please write to us and let us know your thoughts concerning its content.

Consider assisting us in getting this book into the hands of those who would be encouraged and strengthened by its message:

- Recommend it to your friends and loved ones.

- Order additional copies to give as gifts.

- Keep extra copies on hand to loan to others.

If you have not read the author's other works, order them today.

We would be honored to have your fellowship in getting this book freely to those who hunger spiritually. We have daily opportunities to send it to pastors, Sunday school teachers, Bible college professors and students, Bible class teachers, and prisoners.

Do You Subscribe to the Bible Student's Notebook™?

This is a periodical that ...

- Promotes the study of the Bible.
- Encourages the growth of the believer in grace.
- Supports the role of the family patriarch.
- Is dedicated to the recovery of truth that has too long been hidden under the veils of traditionalism, prejudice, misunderstanding and fear.
- Is not connected with any "Movement," "Organization," "Mission," or separate body of believers, but is sent forth to and for all saints.

The *Bible Student's Notebook™* is a *free* electronic publication published weekly (52 times a year).

SUBSCRIBE TODAY!

To receive your *free* electronic subscription, email us at:
bsn@studyshelf.com

By *special order* you may also subscribe to a printed, mailed edition for only $1.00 per issue (to cover production and mailing costs). Example: ½ Year (26 issues) = $26; 1 Year (52 issues) = $52

Bible Student's Notebook™
PO Box 265 Windber, PA 15963
www.BibleStudentsNotebook.com
1-800-784-6010

DAILY EMAIL GOODIES™

Do you receive our
Daily Email Goodies™?

These are free daily emails that contain short quotes, articles, and studies on Biblical themes.

These are the original writings of Clyde L. Pilkington, Jr, as well as gleanings from other authors.

<u>Here is what our readers are saying</u>:

"Profound! Comforting! Calming! Wonderful!" – NC

"The Daily Email Goodies continue to bless my heart! ... They provide plenty of food for thought." – IL

"I really appreciate the Goodies!" – VA

"Your Daily Email Goodies are making me aware of authors whose names I don't even know." – GA

"I am glad to be getting the Daily Email Goodies – keep 'em coming." – IN

Request to be added to our free
Daily Email Goodies™

If you would like to be added to the mailing list, email us at:
Goodies@StudyShelf.com

Believer's Warfare, The: Wearing the Armor of Light in the Darkness of this World

(#7000) The believer is in the middle of an ancient spiritual warfare that is as old as mankind. The battle itself, although intense, is not complicated. It is not a process of spiritual hoop-jumping. Indeed it is simple. The Believer's Warfare surveys a few key passages of Scripture to reveal God's sure plan of victory in the life of His saints. ISBN: 9781934251003 – 48 pages, BK.

Being OK with Not Being OK: Embracing God's Design for You – and Everyone You Know (and Don't Know)

(#1985) For now, you're broken, and you aren't going to be "fixed." Granted, you may have some days that are better than others, some circumstances that seem to indicate that you are "OK," but the wearisome cycle simply will recur.

Thus it is by design – by divine design. Father is bringing you to a place where you are OK with not being OK, where you simply rest in His current purpose and plan in your training and development for that grand and magnificent culmination that He has so wonderfully and skillfully designed especially for you – in your next life. 134 pp., PB. *$9.*^{25}

Bible Student's Notebook, The (VOLUMES)

The Bible Student's Notebook is a periodical dedicated to the: - Promotion of Bible study - Encouragement of the believer's growth in grace - Support of the role of family patriarch - Recovery of truth that has too long been hidden under the veils of traditionalism, prejudice, misunderstanding and fear. The Bible Student's Notebook is not connected with any "Church," "Movement," "Organization," "Society," "Mission," or separate body of believers, but is sent forth to and for all of God's saints. Available in Paperback Volumes.

Church in Ruins, The: Brief Thoughts on II Timothy

(#3325) This brief survey of Paul's last epistle will reveal that, while almost 2000 years have transpired, the condition of the church has remained the same, and indeed has worsened in accordance with Paul's warning to Timothy. This book is not a call for a re-awakening of "the church," because it is apparent that this is not Father's plan. Rather, it is a call to individual men – men whose place in the Christian religious system has left them empty, stagnant and restless – to awaken to Father's call to be His faithful servant and stand outside of that system to look for other faithful men as well. – 128 pages, PB.

Daily Gleanings – 365 Selections on Scriptural Truths

(#1836) This book contains a collection of gleanings from some 200 different authors. These excerpts are intended to be an encouragement to those who are walking on a different path with the Lord – a journey that is *"outside of the camp."*

Some quotations are from beloved and trusted authors, but more often than not, they are from unusual sources. Sometimes, it is simply amazing how an author can admit in print to some grand truth that their writings and ministries otherwise generally deny. For the authors of these quotes, the truth that is conveyed by them may oddly seem "out of place"; but in some ways, the more unlikely the source, the more amazingly it testifies to the truth – and the fact that it cannot be hidden. 253 pp., PB. *$19.*^{25}

Daily Goodies: 365 Thoughts on Scriptural Truths

(#1747) This is a great resource for personal and family study, as well as a valuable reference volume covering many varied biblical themes. This is a collection of choice selections from the author's Daily E-mail Goodies. These free daily e-mails began being issued in 2003 and contain studies on scriptural themes. 490 pp., PB. *$19.*^{25}

Due Benevolence: A Study of Biblical Sexuality

(#3775) Think you have read all that there is on the subject of sexuality from the Bible? Think again! Religious moralists have taken the wonderful gifts of human beauty and sexuality, and made them something dirty and sinful. Much is at stake regarding truth, as well as the nature and character of God Himself. A groundbreaking work providing:

- A refreshingly honest and uninhibited look at sexuality.
- A breath of fresh air from the religious and Victorian mentality.
- A daring and valuable glimpse at the wonderful light just outside sexuality's prison-cell door.
- 220 pages, PB.

God's Holy Nation: Israel and Her Earthly Purpose (Contrasted with the Body of Christ and Its Heavenly Purpose)

(#2275) Israel plays a key role in God's plan of the ages. Though currently she has been set aside "until the times of the nations be fulfi lled," He is by no means done with her.

Today, God is operating His purpose in the ecclesia – the Church, the Body of Christ. The Scriptures provide us with the clear, critical distinction between God's earthly nation and Christ's celestial body.

Christendom, however, has diminished Israel's divine significance in an attempt to advance their artificial homogenization of Scripture's grand theme, thus obscuring the glorious evangel of our day – "the Good News of the Happy God" committed to the trust of Paul, our Apostle.

This work highlights some of the more prominent distinctions which belong to God's literal, physical, earthly nation. In so doing, it is our desire to allow the reader to see more clearly God's dealings with God's favored nation, so that they may in turn embrace a far greater calling and purpose. 360 pp., PB. *$19.*$\underline{^{25}}$

Heaven's Embassy: The Divine Plan & Purpose of the Home

(#5675) The home is central to all of God's dealings with man throughout the course of time. It is His Divine "institution" and "organization" upon the earth, and for the believer, it is the Embassy of Heaven. An embassy is "the residence or office of an ambassador." Since the believer is an ambassador of the Lord Jesus Christ (II Corinthians 5:14-21), his home is thus the Divine Embassy of heavenly ministry. Pauline ministry is centered in the homes of believers. This is even the true sphere of the Body of Christ; for this reason our apostle speaks of "church in thy house." This book doesn't focus upon the external specifics of the ministry of Heaven's Embassy (such as hospitality); that will be saved for another volume. Instead, it looks at the inner-workings of the Embassy itself; focusing upon its very nature and internal purpose and function. – 250 pages, PB.

I Choose! Living Life to Its Fullest

(#4120) Forty-Eight Daily Thoughts on Divine Life. You are alive! Yet not just alive, but alive with the very life of God! Don't allow your "What if …" imaginations of the past or the future to lay claim to the present that God has given you. Allow the objective, unchanging truth of who God has made you in the Lord Jesus Christ to transform your mind and life as you take this spiritual journey of "I Choose." – 192 pages, PB.

I Am! Who and What God Says I Am! The Divine Reckoning of the Renewed Mind; Daily Thoughts on Divine Life

(#1737) People are always talking about their attempts to discover their true selves – of trying to "find themselves." The believer in the Lord Jesus Christ needs to find out who they *really* are. This doesn't need to be such a difficult search. All that is really needed is a careful look at the Scriptures, and a simple faith in the words of who and what God says we are. God knows who we are; all we need to do is to *believe Him.* This book catalogs the Divine Record of who and what God says that you are. It is a short encyclopedia of faith – the truth about you. It is the truth about you, simply because it is *God* Who has said it. God has spoken these truths concerning you – the *real* you. Believe His record! Refuse to be the shell of a person, pushed into a mold of Adamic conformity. Be the real you that God has uniquely designed you to be. Refuse to be bullied out of your divinely designed identity that our Father has given you. 107 pp., PB. *$9.*$^{\underline{25}}$

King James Version, The – 400 Years of Bondage – 1611-2011

(#4682) 1611 was not a high spiritual mark in the history of the church, the Body of Christ. Instead of being a grand year of the pinnacle of preservation or perfection of God's Word, it was rather the sad depths of the subtle corrupting of God's Word by the historic union of governmental and ecclesiastical politics. 72 pp., PB. *$9.*$^{\underline{25}}$

Nothing Will Be Lost! The Truth About God's Good News

(#3750) This is an abridgement of the larger work The Salvation of All. It is designed as a give-away edition, with quantity pricing available. – 88 pages, PB.

Plowboy's Bible, The: God's Word for Common Man

(#4425) Shocking conclusions from the man that brought you The King James Bible Song. This book represents years of study and a significant change in understanding. Raised on and trained in a "King James Only" position, most of the author's teaching ministry was centered on the defense of the KJV. He had early associations with major proponents of this position and their followers. He actively taught classes and seminars on the subject of Bible versions. For many years he distributed thousands of books from a collection of over 100 different titles in support of the KJV position. Here he shares what he has come to see that has caused him to completely abandon his former position. – 254 pages, PB.

Outsiders, The: God's Called-Out Ones – A Biblical Look at the Church – God's Ecclesia

(#4125) In 1995, after sixteen years of being in the "pastorate" the author walked away. He left the "religious system" by resigning from the very "church" and "ministry" he had formed. In many ways this work is a testament to these actions. This testimony was thirty years in the making -- the results of a spiritual journey that the author found to be common to other saints scattered throughout the world and across history. This is an opportunity to explain why some who love the Lord no longer "go to church." It does not seek to persuade others to do something different; but rather to simply be who and what they already are "in Him." This is an uncovering of the truth of the church, and an encouragement for the members of His Body to enjoy the position and standing "in Christ" that they already possess, realizing that they are truly "complete in Him" (Colossians 2:10), that He alone is their Life (Colossians 3:4), and that His Life is full of freedom (Galatians 5:1). 128 pp., PB. *$9.²⁵*

Suffering: God's Forgotten Gift

Two gifts given to the believer are mentioned by Paul in Philippians 1:29. The first is *"to believe on Him."* This is a glorious gift. Every believer has been given this gift from God. Those who possess it may not even fully recognize it as a gift from Him, but indeed faith is God's wonderful gift to us. Faith is a rich gift from God, but there is also another gift from God to the believer mentioned by Paul in Philippians 1:29 that is equally as glorious. The second gift is *"also to suffer for His sake."* This, too, is a glorious gift. Every believer has been

given this gift from God as well, but those who possess it often do not fully recognize it for what it is. Indeed, suffering for His sake similarly is God's wonderful gift to us. Paul teaches us to embrace this second gift as well as we do the first! – 100 pages PB.

Great Omission, The: Christendom's Abandonment of the Biblical Family

(#2010) This book presents twenty years of study, taking a candid look at the issue of multiple wives in Scripture and society. The book chapters are: The Problem; The Divine Provision; The Marital Gift; The Old Testament Scriptural Precedent; The New Testament Scriptural Precedent; The Religious System's Destruction of the Biblical Family; The History of Its Practice; The Cultural Issue. This book also has 14 appendixes. 204 pp., PB. *$14.²⁵*

Salvation Of ALL, The: Creation's Final Destination (A Biblical Look at Universal Reconciliation)

(#7001) The Gospel of our Lord and Savior, Jesus Christ is truly better "Good News" than we could ever have imagined. It is far more glorious than religion would ever have us believe. The Salvation of All is a book about a "Good News" that will reach its final goal in the salvation of all mankind. – 302 pages, PB.

ENJOY BOOKS?

Visit us at:

www.StudyShelf.com

Over the years we have often been asked to recommend books. The requests come from believers who longed for material with substance. Study Shelf™ is a collection of books which are, in our opinion, the very best in print. Many of these books are "unknown" to the members of the Body of Christ at large, and most are not available at your local "Christian" bookstore.

YOU CAN:

Read

A wealth of articles from past issues of the *Bible Student's Notebook* ™

Purchase

Rare and hard to find books, booklets, leaflets, Bibles, etc. in our 24/7 online store.

L - #0078 - 280119 - C0 - 216/140/14 - PB - DID2424329